Hacking the Future:

Exploring the World of Ethical Hacking

By

Annie A. Stringer

TABLE OF CONTENTS

CHAPTER IX
Ethical Hacking for Defense

CHAPTER X

CHAPTER XI

CHAPTER I
Introduction

Understanding the Rise of Ethical Hacking

In the rapidly evolving digital landscape of the 21st century, technology has become an integral part of our daily lives, influencing various aspects of society, business, and governance. With the increasing reliance on interconnected systems and the internet, the vulnerabilities and risks associated with cyber threats have grown exponentially. As our world becomes more dependent on technology, the concept of hacking, once synonymous with malicious activities and cybercrime, has taken a significant turn towards a more constructive and noble purpose – ethical hacking.

In this introductory section of "Hacking the Future: Exploring the World of Ethical Hacking," we embark on a journey to unravel the phenomenon of ethical hacking, understand its emergence, and explore its vital role in securing the digital future. Ethical hacking, also known as penetration testing or white-hat hacking, involves simulating cyberattacks on systems, networks, or applications with the objective of identifying and rectifying vulnerabilities before malicious hackers can exploit them.

The rise of ethical hacking can be traced back to the pioneering work of early computer enthusiasts who sought to understand the intricacies of computing systems and networks. As technology advanced, so did the dark side of hacking, with cybercriminals exploiting weaknesses for personal gain, espionage, and other malicious intentions. This prompted the need for a formidable defense against these threats, and ethical hacking emerged as the solution.

Ethical hackers, armed with extensive knowledge of cybersecurity, employ their skills for constructive purposes – to help individuals, businesses, and governments fortify their defenses against cyber threats. They act as the guardians of digital infrastructure, proactively seeking vulnerabilities that could be exploited by malicious actors. The emergence of ethical hacking is not just a response to the surge in cybercrime; it is a testament to the indomitable spirit of the cybersecurity community to protect and preserve the integrity of the digital world.

As we dive deeper into the world of ethical hacking, we will explore various methodologies, tools, and techniques used by ethical hackers in their pursuit of securing the digital realm. From passive information gathering to active penetration testing, we will uncover the intricacies of how ethical hackers assess and challenge the security posture of organizations.

Beyond the technical aspects, ethical hacking is built on a strong foundation of ethics and legality. The practice emphasizes the importance of obtaining proper authorization before conducting any security assessments. Understanding the legal boundaries is crucial for ensuring that ethical hackers operate within the realms of law and uphold their ethical responsibilities.

Moreover, ethical hacking is not just confined to private organizations or businesses; it has become an essential element of national security and defense. Governments around the world now recognize the significance of ethical hacking in safeguarding critical infrastructure, military systems, and sensitive information from potential cyber threats.

In this book, we aim to shed light on the multifaceted world of ethical hacking. We will delve into the challenges, opportunities, and the ethical implications that come with this dynamic field. As readers journey through the chapters, they will gain insights into the methodologies used by ethical hackers, the significance of their role in shaping cybersecurity policies, and the exciting prospects this domain holds for aspiring cybersecurity professionals.

The exploration of ethical hacking in this book goes beyond the technicalities; it is an exploration of the future – a future where technology and cybersecurity intertwine to create a safer and more secure digital environment. So, let us embark on this expedition into the realm of ethical hacking, where we will witness firsthand how these modern-day digital warriors are hacking the future for the greater good of society.

B. The Importance of Ethical Hacking in Modern Society

In the digital age, where technology permeates every aspect of our lives, the importance of ethical hacking has never been more critical. As our world becomes increasingly interconnected through the internet and digital networks, the potential for cyber threats and attacks has grown exponentially. Ethical hacking plays a pivotal role in safeguarding our modern society from malicious actors and defending against cyber threats that have the potential to disrupt businesses, compromise personal data, and even threaten national security.

One of the primary reasons ethical hacking holds such significance is its proactive approach to cybersecurity. Rather than waiting for cyber attackers to exploit vulnerabilities, ethical hackers take the initiative to identify and address weaknesses before they can be used maliciously. By conducting controlled and authorized security assessments, they expose the very same vulnerabilities that malicious hackers would exploit, but with the intention of fixing them promptly. This approach empowers organizations and individuals to stay one step ahead in the perpetual cat-and-mouse game against cyber threats.

In the corporate world, businesses of all sizes are embracing the concept of ethical hacking to secure their sensitive data, intellectual property, and financial assets. High-profile data breaches and cyberattacks on major companies have demonstrated the devastating consequences of insufficient cybersecurity measures. By engaging ethical hackers to rigorously test their systems, organizations can identify and patch vulnerabilities, protecting their reputation, customer trust, and ultimately, their bottom line.

Moreover, ethical hacking is not confined to the private sector. Governments and public institutions are equally invested in the practice to ensure the security of critical infrastructure and sensitive information. With the rise of cyber warfare and nation-state attacks, ethical hacking has become an indispensable component of national defense. Ethical hackers work alongside intelligence agencies and cybersecurity experts to thwart potential threats, safeguarding the stability and sovereignty of nations in the digital domain.

Beyond the corporate and government sectors, ethical hacking also plays a vital role in securing individuals' online activities. With the increasing use of internet-enabled devices, cybercriminals have ample opportunities to exploit security gaps in personal computers, smartphones, and IoT devices. Ethical hackers help raise awareness among the general public about potential threats and educate them on best practices to stay safe online.

Furthermore, the importance of ethical hacking extends to shaping cybersecurity policies and regulations. As ethical hackers continually uncover new vulnerabilities and risks, they provide valuable insights to lawmakers and industry regulators. These insights help in the development of robust cybersecurity frameworks that keep pace with evolving cyber threats.

Another essential aspect of ethical hacking is its role in fostering a culture of continuous improvement in cybersecurity practices. By identifying weaknesses and promoting best practices, ethical hackers encourage organizations to invest in ongoing cybersecurity training and to maintain a vigilant approach to security. This, in turn, creates a safer digital environment for everyone.

As we progress through this book, we will delve deeper into the different dimensions of ethical hacking, exploring its methodologies, challenges, and future prospects. We will witness the real-world impact of ethical hacking in fortifying organizations against cyber threats and how it contributes to building a resilient and secure digital society.

In conclusion, ethical hacking is not just a technical discipline; it is a crucial force in the ongoing battle for cybersecurity. Its role in protecting businesses, governments, and individuals from the ever-evolving threat landscape cannot be overstated. As we adapt to a world increasingly reliant on technology, ethical hacking remains an indispensable tool, ensuring that our digital future is built on a foundation of security and trust.

C. Defining the Scope of the Book

"Hacking the Future: Exploring the World of Ethical Hacking" sets out on a comprehensive journey to illuminate the intriguing realm of ethical hacking and its profound impact on the modern world. In this section, we define the scope of this book, outlining the key areas and topics that will be covered to provide readers with a well-rounded understanding of ethical hacking and its multifaceted applications.

The primary focus of this book is to demystify ethical hacking and present it as a valuable and constructive approach to cybersecurity. It delves into the methodologies, tools, and techniques employed by ethical hackers to assess and fortify the security of digital systems, networks, and applications. While traditional hacking has often been associated with malicious intent, ethical hacking upholds a noble purpose – to protect individuals, organizations, and nations from the ever-growing threats in cyberspace.

We begin by charting the historical trajectory of hacking, exploring its evolution from a hobbyist pursuit to a menacing criminal activity, ultimately leading to the emergence of ethical hacking as a countermeasure. Understanding the roots of hacking allows us to appreciate the significant shift towards ethical hacking, where skilled cybersecurity professionals wield their expertise to defend against cyber threats.

The book comprehensively covers the essential foundations of ethical hacking, including differentiating ethical hacking from cybercrime. It clarifies the ethical boundaries and legal considerations that ethical hackers must navigate to ensure they operate within the confines of the law while effectively safeguarding digital assets.

An integral aspect of the book involves providing readers with a practical roadmap to becoming a proficient ethical hacker. We explore the fundamental skills, knowledge, and mindset required to embark on a successful ethical hacking journey. Additionally, we highlight the diverse career opportunities available in the field of cybersecurity and ethical hacking.

To equip readers with a holistic understanding of ethical hacking, we explore the vital phases of a typical ethical hacking engagement. From reconnaissance and information gathering to vulnerability assessment and penetration testing, each stage is meticulously examined, along with the latest tools and techniques utilized by ethical hackers.

Moreover, we delve into the real-world applications of ethical hacking in various domains. We uncover how ethical hacking contributes to the security of businesses and organizations, the challenges it poses in securing emerging technologies like IoT and cloud environments, and its indispensable role in protecting critical infrastructures.

The book not only caters to aspiring ethical hackers but also addresses the needs of individuals and organizations looking to strengthen their cybersecurity posture. It provides invaluable insights into implementing effective cybersecurity measures, responding to incidents, and cultivating a security-aware culture.

Ethical hacking is an ever-evolving field, and this book aims to stay ahead of the curve by discussing the latest trends and technologies. We explore cutting-edge concepts like evading intrusion detection systems, advanced persistent threats, reverse engineering, and exploit development, showcasing the frontiers of ethical hacking.

Throughout the book, ethical dilemmas and challenges in the digital landscape are thoughtfully examined. We emphasize the importance of maintaining ethical conduct while practicing ethical hacking and discuss how the global ethical hacking community collaborates to address emerging challenges responsibly.

In conclusion, "Hacking the Future: Exploring the World of Ethical Hacking" provides readers with a comprehensive, insightful, and up-to-date exploration of ethical hacking. Whether you are an aspiring cybersecurity professional, an organization seeking to bolster its defenses, or simply curious about the world of ethical hacking, this book will equip you with the knowledge and understanding needed to navigate the dynamic world of cybersecurity and contribute to securing the digital future.

CHAPTER II
The Foundations of Ethical Hacking

A. A Brief History of Hacking and Its Evolution

To comprehend the essence of ethical hacking, one must first journey back in time to explore the origins and evolution of hacking. Hacking, in its early days, was an innocent pursuit driven by curiosity and a desire to explore the capabilities of early computer systems. As we delve into this brief history, we will witness how this once benign activity took a darker turn, leading to the need for ethical hacking as a powerful defense against cyber threats.

In the late 1950s and 1960s, during the dawn of the computer age, hacking emerged as a hobbyist endeavor at renowned institutions like MIT. Enthusiastic computer scientists and students sought to test the limits of the new computing machines, experimenting with programming and breaking into systems to better understand their inner workings. This early form of hacking was rooted in intellectual curiosity and a sense of adventure, with no malicious intent behind it.

However, as computer technology evolved and became more prevalent in the 1970s and 1980s, hacking began to acquire a darker reputation. The advent of the personal computer brought forth a wave of hackers who exploited vulnerabilities for personal gain or fame. Hacking was no longer confined to academic institutions but spread to online bulletin board systems and early networks, enabling hackers to share their knowledge and techniques more widely.

The 1980s saw the rise of notorious hackers and hacker groups who indulged in illicit activities. The first computer worms and viruses emerged, causing significant disruptions and financial losses. High-profile incidents, such as the Morris Worm in 1988, served as a wake-up call for the potential dangers posed by malicious hacking.

With the proliferation of the internet in the 1990s, hacking took on a global scale. Cybercriminals capitalized on the growing connectivity to launch attacks on businesses, governments, and individuals. Hacking became synonymous with cybercrime, and the term "black hat" hackers emerged to describe those engaging in illegal and malicious activities.

The increasing prevalence of cyber threats in the late 1990s and early 2000s led to a paradigm shift in the cybersecurity landscape. The need for a countermeasure to combat cybercrime became evident, giving rise to the concept of ethical hacking. Ethical hackers, also known as "white hat" hackers, emerged as cybersecurity experts who used their skills for the greater good. Their mission was to identify vulnerabilities in systems, networks, and applications before malicious hackers could exploit them, thereby fortifying defenses and safeguarding digital assets.

In the early 2000s, ethical hacking gained recognition as a legitimate and essential practice. Governments, businesses, and organizations sought the expertise of ethical hackers to assess and enhance their cybersecurity posture. Certification programs, such as Certified Ethical Hacker (CEH), were established to validate the skills of ethical hackers and promote responsible hacking practices.

Today, ethical hacking is an indispensable element of cybersecurity, playing a pivotal role in securing the digital landscape. Ethical hackers continue to contribute to a safer online environment, defending against ever-evolving cyber threats and ensuring that the dark history of hacking is outweighed by the positive impact of ethical hacking in shaping the future of cybersecurity.

B. Differentiating Ethical Hacking from Cybercrime

In the realm of cybersecurity, the lines between ethical hacking and cybercrime can appear blurred to the untrained eye. Both involve penetrating computer systems and networks, but their intentions and methodologies distinguish them starkly. In this section, we explore the fundamental differences between ethical hacking and cybercrime, shedding light on the ethical and legal aspects that guide these practices.

1. Intentions:

The primary and most critical distinction lies in the intentions of the individuals engaging in these activities.

Ethical hacking is conducted with explicit authorization and aims to identify and resolve vulnerabilities to strengthen the security of systems. Ethical hackers operate within a framework of legality and ethics, with the sole purpose of helping individuals, businesses, and governments safeguard their digital assets against potential threats.

On the other hand, cybercrime involves unauthorized access to systems and networks with malicious intent. Cybercriminals exploit vulnerabilities to steal sensitive data, cause disruptions, extort victims, or commit fraud. Their actions are driven by personal gain or a desire to harm others, often leading to severe consequences for the victims and legal repercussions for the perpetrators.

2. Authorization:

Ethical hacking is a well-regulated practice that requires explicit permission from the owners of the systems being tested. Before any assessment is conducted, ethical hackers obtain written consent from the organization or individual responsible for the target network. This ensures that the hacking activities are conducted lawfully and responsibly.

Conversely, cybercrime involves unauthorized access and intrusion into systems without the knowledge or consent of the owners. These activities are not only illegal but also violate the privacy and security of the targeted entities.

3. Legality:

Ethical hacking operates strictly within the bounds of the law, abiding by the relevant cybersecurity and privacy regulations. The legal framework ensures that ethical hackers follow proper procedures, protecting them from prosecution and enabling them to contribute effectively to the security of digital systems.

Cybercrime, being illegal, is subject to prosecution and severe penalties. Engaging in unauthorized hacking activities, distributing malware, or engaging in any form of cyber-attacks is considered criminal behavior, and cybercriminals can face imprisonment and fines upon conviction.

4. Ethical Responsibility:

Ethical hacking places a significant emphasis on ethical responsibilities. Ethical hackers commit to using their skills for the greater good and maintaining the confidentiality of any sensitive information they may encounter during their assessments. They disclose identified vulnerabilities only to the authorized parties, preventing any potential misuse or public exposure of the weaknesses.

Conversely, cybercriminals have no such ethical obligations. They exploit vulnerabilities for personal gain, often without any regard for the consequences to the victims or the broader implications of their actions.

In conclusion, the differentiation between ethical hacking and cybercrime lies in the intentions, authorization, legality, and ethical responsibilities of the actors involved. Ethical hacking is a constructive and essential practice that contributes to the security and resilience of our digital world. By understanding these distinctions, we can appreciate the positive impact ethical hacking has in fortifying cybersecurity defenses and mitigating the risks posed by cybercrime.

C. Ethical Hacking Frameworks and Guidelines

Ethical hacking, as a dynamic and evolving discipline, requires a systematic approach to ensure effectiveness, consistency, and adherence to ethical principles. Ethical hacking frameworks and guidelines provide the necessary structure and methodology for conducting ethical hacking assessments. In this section, we delve into the key ethical hacking frameworks and guidelines used by cybersecurity professionals to perform comprehensive and responsible security evaluations.

1. The Open-Source Security Testing Methodology Manual (OSSTMM):

OSSTMM is a widely recognized and respected framework that outlines a comprehensive methodology for conducting security testing and ethical hacking assessments. It emphasizes a holistic approach, covering various aspects of security testing, including operational security, human security, physical security, and more. OSSTMM emphasizes a controlled and scientific approach to penetration testing, helping ethical hackers avoid unnecessary disruptions while thoroughly assessing security vulnerabilities.

2. The National Institute of Standards and Technology (NIST) Special Publications:

NIST has developed several special publications that offer valuable guidelines for ethical hacking and cybersecurity best practices. Notably, NIST Special Publication 800-115 focuses on information security assessment methods and provides an in-depth overview of penetration testing principles and techniques. Additionally, NIST Special Publication 800-115A offers practical guidelines for conducting penetration testing in cloud computing environments.

3. The Penetration Testing Execution Standard (PTES):

PTES is a comprehensive standard that provides a well-structured and organized approach to penetration testing and ethical hacking. It outlines a series of phases that ethical hackers follow, including pre-engagement, intelligence gathering, vulnerability analysis, exploitation, and post-exploitation. PTES helps ethical hackers maintain consistency and thoroughness in their assessments and ensures that all critical aspects of security testing are covered.

4. The Information Systems Security Assessment Framework (ISSAF):

ISSAF is a methodology designed to guide ethical hackers through the entire process of information systems security assessment. It offers a step-by-step approach, starting from initial scoping and reconnaissance to vulnerability identification, exploitation, and reporting. ISSAF also addresses aspects such as legal considerations, documentation, and communication with stakeholders during the assessment process.

5. The Payment Card Industry Data Security Standard (PCI DSS):

While not exclusively an ethical hacking framework, PCI DSS is a crucial guideline for ethical hackers conducting assessments in organizations that handle credit card transactions. PCI DSS outlines specific security requirements that must be met to ensure the protection of cardholder data. Ethical hackers involved in such assessments must adhere to PCI DSS guidelines to help organizations achieve and maintain compliance with industry regulations.

6. EC-Council Certified Ethical Hacker (CEH) Program:

The CEH program is a widely recognized certification for ethical hackers and provides a comprehensive curriculum covering various aspects of ethical hacking. The program emphasizes hands-on experience, equipping candidates with practical skills and knowledge required for successful ethical hacking assessments. CEH is continually updated to incorporate the latest trends and best practices in the field.

In conclusion, ethical hacking frameworks and guidelines are essential pillars that support the responsible and effective practice of ethical hacking. These frameworks offer a structured and systematic approach, ensuring that ethical hackers conduct assessments in a controlled, thorough, and lawful manner. By adhering to these guidelines, ethical hackers contribute to the overall security and resilience of digital systems and assist organizations in fortifying their defenses against ever-evolving cyber threats.

CHAPTER III
Preparing for the Journey

A. Building a Strong Ethical Hacking Skill Set

Becoming a proficient ethical hacker requires a diverse skill set encompassing technical expertise, problem-solving abilities, and an unwavering commitment to ethical conduct. In this section, we explore the essential skills that aspiring ethical hackers must develop to embark on a successful journey in the world of cybersecurity.

1. Proficiency in Networking:

A strong foundation in networking is crucial for ethical hackers, as most security assessments involve understanding network configurations and communication protocols. Ethical hackers should be well-versed in TCP/IP, subnetting, routing, and firewall technologies to effectively analyze and evaluate network security.

2. Understanding Operating Systems:

Ethical hackers must possess a deep understanding of various operating systems, including Windows, Linux, and macOS. This knowledge enables them to identify vulnerabilities specific to each platform and devise appropriate security measures.

3. Programming Skills:

Proficiency in programming languages is a fundamental requirement for ethical hackers. They should be skilled in languages like Python, Java, C/C++, or scripting languages such as Bash and PowerShell. Programming knowledge aids in creating custom tools and scripts for vulnerability identification and exploitation.

4. Web Application Technologies:

A significant portion of security assessments involves testing web applications for potential vulnerabilities. Ethical hackers should be familiar with web technologies, such as HTML, CSS, JavaScript, and various web application frameworks.

5. Database Knowledge:

Understanding databases and the underlying SQL (Structured Query Language) is essential for assessing web applications and identifying potential flaws in database security.

6. Penetration Testing Techniques:

Ethical hackers must be well-versed in penetration testing techniques, which involve actively simulating cyberattacks on systems to identify security weaknesses. They should understand the methodologies and tools used in penetration testing, such as reconnaissance, scanning, enumeration, and exploitation.

7. Cryptography:

A solid understanding of cryptography is crucial for ethical hackers to assess the security of encrypted data and communications. Knowledge of cryptographic algorithms and protocols helps ethical hackers identify potential weaknesses and recommend stronger cryptographic solutions.

8. Reverse Engineering:

Ethical hackers often encounter malware and suspicious binaries during their assessments. Proficiency in reverse engineering allows them to analyze malware and understand its behavior, aiding in the identification of security risks.

9. Problem-Solving and Analytical Skills:

Ethical hacking involves complex problem-solving and analytical thinking. Ethical hackers must be able to analyze large amounts of data, identify patterns, and deduce potential security vulnerabilities.

10. Continuous Learning and Curiosity:

The cybersecurity landscape is ever-evolving, and ethical hackers must be committed to continuous learning. Staying up-to-date with the latest hacking techniques, security trends, and emerging technologies is essential for maintaining relevance and effectiveness in the field.

In conclusion, building a strong ethical hacking skill set requires dedication, practice, and a thirst for knowledge. Ethical hackers must possess a diverse range of technical competencies to effectively assess and fortify the security of digital systems. Aspiring ethical hackers should focus on honing their networking, programming, web application, and penetration testing skills, while also cultivating problem-solving and analytical thinking abilities. Embracing a mindset of continuous learning and curiosity is pivotal for staying ahead in the dynamic world of cybersecurity and ensuring a successful journey as an ethical hacker.

B. Understanding the Hacker Mindset

To become an effective and successful ethical hacker, it is essential to delve into the intricacies of the hacker mindset. Ethical hackers must possess a unique perspective that combines technical acumen, creativity, and critical thinking. In this section, we explore the fundamental aspects of the hacker mindset and how it influences their approach to ethical hacking.

1. Curiosity and Inquisitiveness:

At the core of the hacker mindset lies an insatiable curiosity and inquisitiveness. Ethical hackers are driven by a relentless desire to understand how systems work, how they can be manipulated, and how vulnerabilities can be exposed. This curiosity fuels their quest for knowledge and encourages them to explore the depths of technology.

2. Problem-Solving Prowess:

Hackers, whether ethical or malicious, are natural problem solvers. They approach challenges with a tenacity to uncover solutions and work tirelessly to break through barriers. Ethical hackers embrace the challenges posed by complex security systems and view them as opportunities to innovate and improve.

3. A Creative Approach:

Ethical hackers think outside the box and possess a creative mindset. They are not bound by conventional methods and are open to unconventional techniques to identify and exploit vulnerabilities. This creativity enables them to simulate diverse attack scenarios, ensuring a thorough security assessment.

4. Persistence and Resilience:

Hacking, even in an ethical context, is not always straightforward. Ethical hackers face numerous obstacles and setbacks during their assessments. The ability to persist through challenges and bounce back from failures is a hallmark of the hacker mindset. They embrace failure as a stepping stone to success and continuously refine their strategies.

5. Continuous Learning:

Ethical hackers thrive on knowledge and continuously seek to expand their skills. They keep abreast of the latest hacking techniques, security trends, and emerging technologies to stay ahead of cyber threats. The pursuit of knowledge is a lifelong endeavor for ethical hackers, and they understand that learning is key to success in the ever-changing cybersecurity landscape.

6. Ethical Responsibility:

While hackers may be associated with subversive behavior, ethical hackers embrace a strong sense of responsibility. They understand the potential consequences of their actions and are dedicated to using their skills for the greater good. The ethical hacker mindset entails operating within legal boundaries and upholding strict ethical standards in all their assessments.

7. White Hat Collaboration:

Ethical hackers are part of a global community of cybersecurity professionals known as white hat hackers. Collaboration and knowledge-sharing among ethical hackers are widespread, as they understand the collective strength in addressing cyber threats. This spirit of cooperation enables them to learn from each other, pool resources, and contribute to the overall cybersecurity landscape.

8. Empathy and User-Centric Focus:

Ethical hackers empathize with end-users and strive to protect them from potential harm. They place the end-users' interests and security at the forefront of their assessments. This user-centric approach helps ethical hackers identify vulnerabilities that may directly impact individuals' privacy and data protection.

In conclusion, understanding the hacker mindset is crucial for aspiring ethical hackers. This unique perspective combines curiosity, problem-solving prowess, creativity, and resilience. Ethical hackers continuously seek knowledge, uphold ethical responsibilities, and collaborate within the white hat community. Their user-centric focus ensures that their work contributes to a safer digital environment for individuals and organizations. By embracing the hacker mindset, ethical hackers lay the foundation for successful security assessments and a meaningful career in cybersecurity.

C. Ethics and Legal Considerations in Ethical Hacking

Ethical hacking, despite its noble intent, operates in a delicate balance between legality and responsibility. Aspiring ethical hackers must be well-versed in the ethical principles and legal considerations that govern their practice. In this section, we explore the critical ethics and legal aspects that ethical hackers must consider before embarking on their cybersecurity journey.

1. Informed Consent:

Obtaining informed consent is a fundamental ethical principle in ethical hacking. Before conducting any security assessments, ethical hackers must seek explicit permission from the owners of the systems or networks being tested. This ensures that the hacking activities are authorized and align with ethical boundaries.

2. Scope of Assessment:

Ethical hackers must clearly define the scope of their assessments in consultation with the organizations they are working with. Defining the scope prevents unintentional disruptions and ensures that the focus remains on specific targets, minimizing any unintended consequences.

3. Confidentiality and Data Privacy:

Respecting confidentiality and data privacy is paramount in ethical hacking. Ethical hackers may encounter sensitive information during their assessments, and it is their ethical duty to handle such data with the utmost confidentiality. Any findings or reports must be communicated only to authorized stakeholders and never publicly disclosed without consent.

4. Avoiding Harm:

Ethical hackers must take all precautions to avoid causing harm during their assessments. While their intent is to identify vulnerabilities, any unintended damage to systems or networks should be minimized. Ethical hackers must exercise caution to prevent disruptions that could impact business operations.

5. Non-Disclosure Agreements (NDAs):

In some cases, ethical hackers may be required to sign non-disclosure agreements before conducting security assessments. NDAs legally bind ethical hackers to maintain the confidentiality of the assessment process and findings, ensuring that sensitive information remains secure.

6. Compliance with Laws and Regulations:

Ethical hackers must be well-informed about relevant cybersecurity laws, regulations, and industry standards. Adhering to these legal frameworks ensures that their activities remain within the bounds of the law and safeguards them from potential legal repercussions.

7. Reporting Vulnerabilities Responsibly:

When ethical hackers discover vulnerabilities, they must report their findings responsibly. This involves promptly notifying the affected parties and providing clear, actionable recommendations for remediation. Responsible reporting helps organizations address security weaknesses and prevent potential exploitation by malicious actors.

8. Continuous Ethical Review:

Ethical hacking is a dynamic field with evolving ethical challenges. Ethical hackers must continually evaluate the ethical implications of their work and adapt their practices accordingly. Embracing a culture of ethical review ensures that ethical hackers maintain their commitment to responsible and lawful hacking.

9. Personal Integrity and Professional Conduct:

Ethical hackers should embody personal integrity and maintain the highest standards of professional conduct. Upholding ethical principles is not limited to hacking activities but extends to all interactions within the cybersecurity community and beyond.

In conclusion, ethics and legal considerations are at the core of ethical hacking. Aspiring ethical hackers must embrace the principles of informed consent, confidentiality, data privacy, and responsible reporting.

Adhering to legal frameworks, conducting assessments within defined scopes, and avoiding unintended harm are essential elements of ethical hacking practice. By upholding ethical standards and fostering a culture of responsible hacking, ethical hackers contribute to a safer digital world and earn the trust of organizations and individuals seeking their cybersecurity expertise.

CHAPTER IV
Reconnaissance and Information Gathering

A. Passive Information Gathering Techniques

Reconnaissance and information gathering form the foundational stage of ethical hacking assessments. Passive information gathering techniques enable ethical hackers to acquire valuable insights about their target systems, networks, and organizations without directly engaging with them. In this section, we explore the essential passive information gathering techniques employed by ethical hackers to gather intelligence discreetly.

1. Open-Source Intelligence (OSINT):

Open-source intelligence is a crucial passive information gathering technique that leverages publicly available information from various sources. Ethical hackers scour websites, social media platforms, forums, and other online resources to extract valuable data about the target organization. OSINT provides details about the organization's structure, employees, partners, and technology stack, aiding ethical hackers in identifying potential attack vectors.

2. Domain Name System (DNS) Enumeration:

DNS enumeration involves querying DNS servers to obtain information about the target's domain names and their associated IP addresses. Ethical hackers use tools like "nslookup" and "dig" to extract DNS records, which can reveal subdomains and other critical information, assisting in the mapping of the target's network infrastructure.

3. WHOIS Lookup:

Performing a WHOIS lookup allows ethical hackers to access domain registration information, such as the domain owner's contact details, registration dates, and nameservers. This information can be valuable in understanding the organization's web presence and infrastructure.

4. Search Engine Hacking (Google Dorking):

Google Dorking involves using advanced search operators on search engines like Google to pinpoint sensitive or vulnerable information inadvertently exposed on the internet. Ethical hackers use carefully crafted search queries to identify files, directories, or login pages that might provide entry points for potential attacks.

5. Email Footprinting:

Email footprinting involves analyzing email headers and sender information to gain insights into the target's email infrastructure and communication patterns. This information may expose email server details and potential weaknesses that can be exploited in phishing attacks.

6. Social Engineering Techniques:

Though not directly passive, social engineering can be employed passively through information gathered from public sources. Ethical hackers analyze the target's social media presence and other publicly available data to identify potential weak links, such as employees susceptible to manipulation, which can be leveraged in later stages of the assessment.

7. Network Enumeration through Publicly Available Tools:

Ethical hackers utilize various network enumeration tools like "Shodan" and "Censys" to passively scan for exposed network devices and services. These tools reveal information about open ports, banners, and service versions, offering insights into potential vulnerabilities.

8. Footprinting from Internet Archive:

The Internet Archive, also known as the Wayback Machine, allows ethical hackers to access historical snapshots of websites. Analyzing past versions of the target's website can reveal forgotten pages, deprecated technologies, and other valuable information.

In conclusion, passive information gathering techniques serve as the initial step in ethical hacking assessments. Ethical hackers rely on open-source intelligence, DNS enumeration, WHOIS lookups, Google Dorking, email footprinting, and social engineering analysis to discreetly gather valuable intelligence about their targets. Utilizing publicly available tools and resources, ethical hackers gain insights into the target's infrastructure, vulnerabilities, and potential attack vectors, laying the groundwork for subsequent stages of the assessment. Ethical hacking operates within ethical and legal boundaries, ensuring that the information gathered is used responsibly and for the purpose of fortifying cybersecurity defenses.

B. Active Information Gathering Techniques

Active information gathering techniques involve direct interaction with the target systems and networks, providing ethical hackers with more comprehensive and real-time insights. Unlike passive techniques, active techniques may leave traces in logs and can potentially cause disruptions if not executed carefully. In this section, we explore the essential active information gathering techniques employed by ethical hackers in their cybersecurity assessments.

1. Port Scanning:

Port scanning is a crucial active technique used to identify open ports on the target system or network. Ethical hackers utilize tools like "Nmap" to send packets to target hosts, probing for open ports and services. Understanding the open ports helps in identifying potential entry points and vulnerabilities.

2. Network Discovery and Enumeration:

Ethical hackers actively probe the target network to discover hosts, network topology, and devices. Techniques like "ARP (Address Resolution Protocol) scanning" and "ping sweeps" enable ethical hackers to identify active hosts on the network, aiding in the mapping of the target's infrastructure.

3. Vulnerability Scanning:

Vulnerability scanning involves using automated tools like "Nessus" or "OpenVAS" to assess the target systems and identify known vulnerabilities. Ethical hackers analyze the scan results to understand potential weaknesses that can be exploited in subsequent stages of the assessment.

4. Banner Grabbing:

Banner grabbing is the process of actively retrieving banners or service information from target systems. Ethical hackers utilize tools like "Telnet" or specialized banner grabbing tools to gather information about running services, including service versions and software information.

5. Active Web Application Scanning:

Ethical hackers employ web application scanning tools like "Burp Suite" or "OWASP ZAP" to actively analyze web applications for security vulnerabilities. These tools simulate attacks on web applications to identify potential weaknesses, such as SQL injection, cross-site scripting (XSS), and insecure configurations.

6. Directory and File Enumeration:

Ethical hackers actively enumerate directories and files on web servers to identify hidden or sensitive resources.

Tools like "DirBuster" and "Gobuster" help in systematically exploring directories, revealing potential misconfigurations or exposed files.

7. DNS Enumeration:

Active DNS enumeration involves querying DNS servers for various records like "A" (Address), "MX" (Mail Exchange), and "NS" (Name Server) records. Ethical hackers utilize tools like "DNSRecon" to gather detailed information about the target's DNS infrastructure.

8. Password Guessing and Brute-Force Attacks:

Password guessing and brute-force attacks are active techniques used to assess the strength of passwords. Ethical hackers use tools like "Hydra" or "Medusa" to attempt to gain unauthorized access to target systems by systematically guessing passwords.

9. Exploitation of Known Vulnerabilities:

In cases where explicit permission is granted and all safety measures are followed, ethical hackers may actively exploit known vulnerabilities to validate their existence and demonstrate the potential impact to the target organization.

In conclusion, active information gathering techniques allow ethical hackers to interact directly with the target systems and networks, providing a more comprehensive assessment of potential vulnerabilities. Ethical hackers use port scanning, network discovery, vulnerability scanning, banner grabbing, web application scanning, and other active techniques to identify and assess security weaknesses. The use of these techniques requires caution and explicit authorization to avoid unintended disruptions and ensure ethical conduct throughout the assessment process. By employing active information gathering techniques responsibly, ethical hackers play a crucial role in helping organizations identify and address security risks, strengthening cybersecurity defenses in an ever-evolving digital landscape.

C. Open-Source Intelligence (OSINT) Tools and Methodologies

Open-Source Intelligence (OSINT) is a powerful reconnaissance technique that allows ethical hackers to gather information from publicly available sources to gain insights about their target organizations. OSINT provides a wealth of data without directly engaging with the target, making it an invaluable first step in ethical hacking assessments. In this section, we explore the OSINT tools and methodologies that ethical hackers utilize to gather intelligence effectively.

1. Google and Other Search Engines:

Google is a primary OSINT tool used by ethical hackers for information gathering. By leveraging advanced search operators, ethical hackers can refine search queries to pinpoint specific information about the target. Other search engines like Bing and Shodan are also valuable in extracting data from various sources.

2. Social Media Platforms:

Social media platforms, such as Facebook, Twitter, LinkedIn, and Instagram, are goldmines of information for ethical hackers. Publicly available profiles and posts provide insights into the target organization's employees, partners, technologies, and interactions, aiding in constructing a comprehensive profile of the target.

3. Web Scraping Tools:

Web scraping tools like "Scrapy" and "Beautiful Soup" assist ethical hackers in extracting data from websites systematically. These tools enable the automated collection of information, such as email addresses, contact details, and other valuable data available on web pages.

4. Domain and WHOIS Lookup Tools:

Domain and WHOIS lookup tools allow ethical hackers to obtain domain registration information, including domain ownership details, registration dates, and nameservers. WHOIS information is valuable in understanding the target's web presence and infrastructure.

5. Email Harvesting Tools:

Email harvesting tools aid ethical hackers in extracting email addresses from websites and public sources. These tools enable the identification of email patterns and potential contact points within the target organization.

6. Data Breach Databases:

Data breach databases, such as "Have I Been Pwned" and "BreachAlarm," provide information about past data breaches affecting the target organization. Ethical hackers use these databases to understand potential security risks and compromised credentials associated with the target.

7. OSINT Frameworks:

Ethical hackers often leverage OSINT frameworks like "Maltego," "Recon-ng," and "theHarvester" to streamline the information gathering process. These frameworks offer a collection of OSINT tools and techniques, enabling ethical hackers to perform thorough reconnaissance efficiently.

8. Wayback Machine:

The Internet Archive's Wayback Machine allows ethical hackers to access historical snapshots of websites. Analyzing past versions of the target's website can reveal deprecated technologies, changes in web structure, and potentially forgotten pages that may provide useful insights.

9. Geolocation Tools:

Geolocation tools like "Geopy" and "MaxMind" assist ethical hackers in determining the physical locations of IP addresses and domains. This information can be valuable in mapping the target organization's digital infrastructure.

In conclusion, OSINT is a valuable set of tools and methodologies for ethical hackers to gather intelligence about their target organizations discreetly. By utilizing Google and other search engines, social media platforms, web scraping tools, domain and WHOIS lookup tools, and data breach databases, ethical hackers gain valuable information for their assessments. OSINT frameworks, email harvesting tools, the Wayback Machine, and geolocation tools further enhance the efficiency and effectiveness of OSINT techniques. It is essential for ethical hackers to practice responsible OSINT, ensuring that the information gathered is used ethically and within the legal boundaries of the assessment. By mastering OSINT, ethical hackers lay a solid foundation for their ethical hacking journey, helping organizations enhance their cybersecurity defenses and protect their digital assets.

CHAPTER V
Vulnerability Assessment and Analysis

A. Identifying System Vulnerabilities

Vulnerability assessment and analysis form a critical phase in the ethical hacking process. Identifying system vulnerabilities is essential for ethical hackers to understand the weaknesses that malicious actors could potentially exploit. In this section, we explore the methodologies and tools used by ethical hackers to identify vulnerabilities in target systems.

1. Automated Vulnerability Scanners:

Automated vulnerability scanners are powerful tools that streamline the process of identifying common security weaknesses. Ethical hackers use tools like "Nessus," "OpenVAS," and "Qualys" to conduct comprehensive scans of the target's systems and networks. These scanners detect known vulnerabilities in operating systems, applications, and services, providing a detailed report of potential weaknesses.

2. Manual Configuration Reviews:

Ethical hackers perform manual configuration reviews to assess the security of various system components. They analyze configurations of operating systems, firewalls, routers, and web servers to identify misconfigurations that might expose critical assets to potential attacks.

3. Password Auditing:

Password auditing is a vital aspect of identifying vulnerabilities in authentication mechanisms. Ethical hackers use tools like "John the Ripper" and "Hashcat" to crack passwords or perform brute-force attacks on hashed passwords. Weak or easily guessable passwords are flagged as security risks.

4. Fuzz Testing (Fuzzing):

Fuzz testing involves sending unexpected and random inputs to applications to discover potential vulnerabilities, such as buffer overflows or input validation flaws. Ethical hackers utilize fuzzing tools like "AFL" (American Fuzzy Lop) and "Peach Fuzzer" to identify programmatic weaknesses that might lead to security breaches.

5. Web Application Security Scanners:

Web application security scanners, like "Burp Suite," "OWASP ZAP," and "Acunetix," focus specifically on identifying vulnerabilities in web applications. These tools simulate attacks on web applications to detect issues like SQL injection, cross-site scripting (XSS), and insecure configurations.

6. Network Vulnerability Scanners:

Network vulnerability scanners, like "Nmap" and "OpenVAS," help ethical hackers discover vulnerabilities in networked devices, including open ports, weak services, and outdated protocols. These scanners provide a comprehensive view of the target's network security posture.

7. Manual Code Reviews:

For custom applications and software, ethical hackers perform manual code reviews. By analyzing source code, ethical hackers can uncover programming errors and security vulnerabilities that might not be detected by automated tools.

8. Protocol Analysis:

Protocol analysis involves examining network traffic to identify potential weaknesses in communication protocols. Ethical hackers use tools like "Wireshark" to capture and analyze packets, helping them uncover vulnerabilities related to insecure communication.

9. Patch Analysis:

Ethical hackers review the target's systems for missing security patches and updates. Exploiting known vulnerabilities that have not been patched is a common tactic used by attackers, making patch analysis crucial in vulnerability identification.

In conclusion, identifying system vulnerabilities is a crucial step in ethical hacking assessments. Ethical hackers employ a variety of methodologies and tools, such as automated vulnerability scanners, manual configuration reviews, password auditing, fuzz testing, web application security scanners, network vulnerability scanners, manual code reviews, protocol analysis, and patch analysis. The combination of automated and manual techniques ensures a thorough and accurate assessment of potential security weaknesses. Ethical hackers meticulously analyze their findings to provide actionable insights and recommendations to organizations, helping them strengthen their cybersecurity defenses and mitigate the risks posed by potential attackers. By conducting vulnerability assessments with precision and expertise, ethical hackers play a crucial role in enhancing the overall security posture of organizations and safeguarding their digital assets.

B. Network Scanning and Enumeration

Network scanning and enumeration are critical phases in the vulnerability assessment process. These techniques allow ethical hackers to gather detailed information about the target's network infrastructure and identify potential entry points and security vulnerabilities. In this section, we explore the methodologies and tools used by ethical hackers for network scanning and enumeration.

1. Port Scanning:

Port scanning is a fundamental network scanning technique used by ethical hackers to discover open ports on target hosts. Ethical hackers utilize tools like "Nmap" to send packets to target hosts and analyze the responses to determine which ports are open and which services are running. Understanding open ports is essential for identifying potential attack vectors and services that might be vulnerable to exploitation.

2. Service Version Detection:

Service version detection complements port scanning by identifying the specific versions of services running on open ports. Ethical hackers use techniques like banner grabbing to retrieve service banners from target hosts, revealing valuable information about the running services and their potential vulnerabilities.

3. Network Mapping and Topology Discovery:

Ethical hackers perform network mapping and topology discovery to gain insights into the target's network structure. Techniques like "ARP scanning" and "ping sweeps" help identify active hosts on the network, assisting in the creation of a network map that shows the relationships between devices and their IP addresses.

4. Operating System Fingerprinting:

Operating system fingerprinting is the process of determining the operating system running on target hosts. Ethical hackers use tools like "Nmap" and "p0f" to analyze network responses and identify the OS based on unique characteristics in the network packets. Knowledge of the operating system aids in understanding potential vulnerabilities specific to that platform.

5. Enumeration of Network Services:

Network service enumeration involves actively querying services on target hosts to gather information about users, shares, and other resources. Ethical hackers use tools like "Enum4linux" for Windows environments and

"Enum" for Linux environments to enumerate information that might be useful in later stages of the assessment.

6. SNMP Enumeration:

Simple Network Management Protocol (SNMP) enumeration is employed to gather information about network devices, such as routers, switches, and printers. Ethical hackers use SNMP tools like "SNMPWalk" to query SNMP-enabled devices for information like system details and configurations.

7. DNS Enumeration:

DNS enumeration involves querying DNS servers for various types of DNS records, such as "A" (Address), "MX" (Mail Exchange), and "NS" (Name Server) records. Ethical hackers use tools like "DNSRecon" to gather detailed information about the target's DNS infrastructure.

8. Directory and File Enumeration:

Directory and file enumeration are techniques used in web applications to identify hidden or sensitive resources. Ethical hackers use tools like "DirBuster" and "Gobuster" to systematically explore directories and find files that might reveal potential security weaknesses.

9. Vulnerability Scanning for Network Devices:

In addition to vulnerability scanning for systems, ethical hackers also scan network devices, such as routers and switches, for known vulnerabilities. Vulnerable network devices can serve as potential entry points for attackers, making it essential to identify and address weaknesses in these devices.

In conclusion, network scanning and enumeration are essential components of vulnerability assessments. Ethical hackers employ port scanning, service version detection, network mapping, operating system fingerprinting, enumeration of network services, SNMP enumeration, DNS enumeration, directory and file enumeration, and vulnerability scanning for network devices to gather detailed information about the target's network infrastructure. These techniques enable ethical hackers to understand the target's network architecture, identify potential security weaknesses, and take proactive measures to bolster cybersecurity defenses. By leveraging network scanning and enumeration effectively, ethical hackers play a crucial role in safeguarding organizations from potential cyber threats and maintaining a robust security posture in today's complex and ever-changing digital landscape.

C. Vulnerability Scanning Tools

Vulnerability scanning is a pivotal aspect of ethical hacking, allowing professionals to systematically identify known weaknesses in target systems and networks. Ethical hackers leverage specialized vulnerability scanning tools to streamline the assessment process and provide comprehensive reports on potential security risks. In this section, we explore some of the popular vulnerability scanning tools utilized by ethical hackers for effective vulnerability assessment.

1. Nessus:

Nessus is one of the most widely used and respected vulnerability scanners in the cybersecurity community. It offers an extensive database of known vulnerabilities and supports a wide range of platforms and operating systems. Ethical hackers can configure scans to target specific assets and receive detailed reports, including severity ratings and remediation recommendations.

2. OpenVAS:

OpenVAS (Open Vulnerability Assessment System) is an open-source vulnerability scanner that provides a comprehensive suite of tools for vulnerability assessment. It offers a user-friendly web interface, making it accessible to both beginners and experienced professionals. OpenVAS is known for its constant updates to the vulnerability database, ensuring up-to-date scanning capabilities.

3. Qualys Vulnerability Management:

Qualys Vulnerability Management is a cloud-based vulnerability scanner widely used by organizations for continuous monitoring of their assets. Ethical hackers can use Qualys to perform remote scans on cloud-based and on-premises infrastructure. The platform offers detailed reporting, asset tagging, and integration with various other security tools.

4. Rapid7 Nexpose:

Rapid7 Nexpose is a vulnerability management solution designed to assess and prioritize risks across dynamic environments. Ethical hackers can schedule regular scans, tailor them to specific assets, and receive real-time alerts for newly discovered vulnerabilities. Nexpose also integrates with various security tools for seamless vulnerability management.

5. Acunetix:

Acunetix is a powerful web application security scanner used to identify vulnerabilities in web applications and

APIs. Ethical hackers can perform in-depth scans for common web vulnerabilities, such as SQL injection and cross-site scripting (XSS), and receive detailed reports with proof-of-concept examples.

6. Burp Suite:

While primarily known as a web application security testing tool, Burp Suite includes a scanner that performs automated vulnerability scans on web applications. Ethical hackers can use Burp Suite's scanning capabilities alongside its proxy and manual testing features for comprehensive web application assessment.

7. OpenSCAP:

OpenSCAP (Security Content Automation Protocol) is an open-source vulnerability scanner that focuses on compliance checking and vulnerability assessment. It is particularly useful for organizations seeking to meet specific security compliance requirements.

8. Nikto:

Nikto is a free and open-source web server scanner used by ethical hackers to detect potential vulnerabilities in web servers and web applications. It performs a wide range of tests, including server misconfigurations, outdated software, and common vulnerabilities.

9. Microsoft Baseline Security Analyzer (MBSA):

MBSA is a free vulnerability scanner developed by Microsoft for Windows-based systems. Ethical hackers can use MBSA to scan for missing security updates, weak passwords, and other security misconfigurations in Windows operating systems.

In conclusion, vulnerability scanning tools are essential components of ethical hacking assessments, allowing professionals to identify known weaknesses in target systems and networks. Nessus, OpenVAS, Qualys Vulnerability Management, Rapid7 Nexpose, Acunetix, Burp Suite, OpenSCAP, Nikto, and Microsoft Baseline Security Analyzer are some of the popular tools used by ethical hackers for comprehensive vulnerability assessment. These tools provide in-depth scanning capabilities, detailed reports, and valuable insights to help organizations fortify their cybersecurity defenses and protect their digital assets from potential threats. Ethical hackers leverage these tools responsibly to conduct thorough assessments, deliver actionable recommendations, and play a crucial role in enhancing the overall security posture of organizations in an ever-evolving digital landscape.

CHAPTER VI
Exploitation and Penetration Testing

A. Exploiting Common System Vulnerabilities

In the realm of ethical hacking, exploitation and penetration testing form the hands-on phase where ethical hackers attempt to verify the real-world impact of identified vulnerabilities. This phase is crucial for organizations to understand the potential consequences of security weaknesses and take proactive measures to strengthen their defenses. In this section, we explore the methodologies used by ethical hackers to exploit common system vulnerabilities during penetration testing.

1. Buffer Overflow Attacks:

Buffer overflow attacks are prevalent in software and applications that do not properly handle input data. Ethical hackers craft malicious input to overflow the buffer and overwrite adjacent memory, leading to the execution of arbitrary code or system crashes. These attacks help identify and address inadequate input validation in applications.

2. SQL Injection (SQLi):

SQL injection is a notorious vulnerability in web applications where attackers insert malicious SQL queries into input fields to manipulate the underlying database. Ethical hackers use SQL injection techniques to gain unauthorized access, extract sensitive data, or even modify database records. Testing for SQL injection helps organizations secure their web applications and prevent data breaches.

3. Cross-Site Scripting (XSS):

Cross-Site Scripting is a vulnerability that allows attackers to inject malicious scripts into web applications viewed by other users. Ethical hackers use XSS to demonstrate potential risks, such as stealing user credentials, session hijacking, or performing other malicious actions on behalf of the user.

4. Remote Code Execution (RCE):

Remote Code Execution vulnerabilities allow attackers to execute code on a target system remotely. Ethical hackers simulate RCE scenarios to assess the severity of the vulnerability and demonstrate how attackers could gain full control over the target system.

5. Privilege Escalation:

Privilege escalation involves exploiting vulnerabilities that allow an attacker to elevate their privileges within the system or network. Ethical hackers seek to escalate privileges to demonstrate the potential impact on data confidentiality and system integrity.

6. Directory Traversal Attacks:

Directory traversal attacks exploit vulnerabilities in web applications to access files and directories outside the intended scope. Ethical hackers use these attacks to demonstrate unauthorized access to sensitive files or system configuration information.

7. Authentication Bypass:

Ethical hackers attempt to bypass authentication mechanisms to access restricted areas or resources. Testing for authentication bypass helps organizations assess the effectiveness of their access control measures.

8. Man-in-the-Middle (MitM) Attacks:

MitM attacks involve intercepting and potentially modifying communication between two parties. Ethical hackers simulate MitM attacks to assess the security of network communications and identify weaknesses in encryption protocols.

9. Denial of Service (DoS) Attacks:

Denial of Service attacks aim to overwhelm a target system or network, rendering it inaccessible to legitimate users. Ethical hackers conduct DoS testing to assess the resilience of systems and identify potential performance bottlenecks.

In conclusion, exploiting common system vulnerabilities during penetration testing is essential for ethical hackers to verify the real-world impact of identified weaknesses. Buffer overflow attacks, SQL injection, Cross-Site Scripting (XSS), Remote Code Execution (RCE), privilege escalation, directory traversal attacks, authentication bypass, Man-in-the-Middle (MitM) attacks, and Denial of Service (DoS) attacks are some of the methodologies used by ethical hackers to demonstrate potential security risks. Through ethical exploitation, organizations gain valuable insights into their security weaknesses and can take proactive measures to enhance their cybersecurity defenses. Ethical hackers play a crucial role in safeguarding digital assets and protecting organizations from malicious actors by conducting thorough and responsible penetration testing assessments.

B. Web Application Penetration Testing

Web applications are a crucial component of modern businesses, and their security is of utmost importance. Web application penetration testing, also known as ethical hacking of web applications, is a specialized process where ethical hackers systematically assess the security of web-based systems and identify potential vulnerabilities. In this section, we delve into the methodologies used by ethical hackers during web application penetration testing to ensure the robustness of these critical assets.

1. Discovery and Reconnaissance:

The initial phase involves information gathering about the web application, its functionalities, and the underlying technologies. Ethical hackers use tools like "Burp Suite" and "OWASP ZAP" to map out the application's attack surface, identify entry points, and understand the application's architecture.

2. Web Application Scanning:

During this phase, ethical hackers utilize automated web application scanners, such as "Acunetix," "Netsparker," and "AppScan," to perform comprehensive vulnerability scans. The scanners simulate various attacks, including SQL injection, XSS, and directory traversal, to identify potential security weaknesses.

3. Manual Testing of Input Fields:

Ethical hackers manually test each input field within the web application to ensure that data is validated and sanitized correctly. By crafting malicious input, they aim to bypass security measures and discover vulnerabilities like SQL injection and Cross-Site Scripting (XSS).

4. Authentication and Authorization Testing:

Ethical hackers assess the web application's authentication and authorization mechanisms to verify their effectiveness. They attempt to bypass authentication controls, escalate privileges, or access unauthorized resources to evaluate the application's access control measures.

5. Session Management Testing:

Session management vulnerabilities can lead to unauthorized access and session hijacking. Ethical hackers evaluate session tokens, cookies, and expiration mechanisms to ensure secure session management.

6. Business Logic Testing:

This phase involves evaluating the business logic of the web application to identify potential flaws that could allow attackers to manipulate transactions or access sensitive data.

7. File Upload Testing:

File upload functionalities can be abused to upload malicious files or execute arbitrary code. Ethical hackers test this functionality to ensure secure file handling and prevent potential security breaches.

8. Error Handling and Information Disclosure:

Error messages and information disclosed by the application can provide valuable insights to attackers. Ethical hackers examine error messages to ensure they do not reveal sensitive information and that they are adequately handled.

9. Security Headers and Configuration Review:

Ethical hackers review security headers, such as Content Security Policy (CSP) and HTTP Strict Transport Security

(HSTS), to enforce security policies and enhance the application's resilience against attacks.

10. Reporting and Remediation:

After conducting the penetration test, ethical hackers compile a comprehensive report detailing the vulnerabilities discovered, their potential impact, and actionable remediation recommendations. This report enables organizations to prioritize and address security weaknesses effectively.

In conclusion, web application penetration testing is a vital process for ensuring the security of web-based systems. Ethical hackers use a combination of automated scanning tools, manual testing techniques, and their expertise to identify vulnerabilities like SQL injection, XSS, authentication bypass, and more. By conducting thorough and meticulous penetration tests, ethical hackers help organizations strengthen their web application security, protect user data, and maintain customer trust. Web application penetration testing is an ongoing and iterative process, empowering businesses to stay ahead of potential threats in the dynamic and ever-changing cybersecurity landscape.

C. Social Engineering Techniques

Social engineering is a psychological manipulation tactic employed by ethical hackers to exploit human behavior and gain unauthorized access to sensitive information, systems, or networks. It is a crucial aspect of penetration testing as attackers often target employees and individuals to circumvent technical security measures. In this section, we delve into the social engineering techniques used by ethical hackers to assess an organization's vulnerability to human-based attacks.

1. Phishing Attacks:

Phishing is one of the most prevalent social engineering techniques. Ethical hackers craft convincing emails, messages, or websites that appear legitimate to trick individuals into revealing confidential information, such as usernames, passwords, or financial details. Phishing campaigns help organizations evaluate their employees' susceptibility to falling for such scams.

2. Spear Phishing:

Spear phishing is a targeted form of phishing that involves personalized and tailored messages aimed at specific individuals or departments. Ethical hackers conduct spear phishing tests to assess the level of awareness and vigilance among employees regarding highly customized attacks.

3. Pretexting:

Pretexting involves creating a fabricated scenario or pretext to manipulate individuals into revealing sensitive information or performing certain actions. Ethical hackers use pretexting techniques to impersonate trusted individuals or organizations, gaining the target's trust and obtaining valuable information.

4. Baiting:

Baiting is a social engineering technique where attackers offer something enticing, such as free software or USB drives, to lure individuals into performing a specific action, like inserting an infected USB drive into a company computer. Ethical hackers conduct baiting tests to evaluate whether employees adhere to security policies regarding the use of external media.

5. Tailgating (Piggybacking):

Tailgating occurs when an unauthorized person gains physical access to a restricted area by following an authorized individual. Ethical hackers test the effectiveness of physical security measures by attempting to tailgate employees into secure areas without proper identification.

6. Dumpster Diving:

Dumpster diving involves rummaging through discarded documents or materials to find sensitive information. Ethical hackers conduct dumpster diving tests to assess whether organizations dispose of confidential data securely and whether employees are aware of the risks.

7. Impersonation:

Ethical hackers attempt to impersonate legitimate employees or contractors to gain access to secure areas or sensitive information. This technique evaluates an organization's ability to recognize and respond to unauthorized individuals attempting to gain physical access.

8. Vishing (Voice Phishing):

Vishing is a social engineering technique that uses phone calls to deceive individuals into revealing sensitive information or performing certain actions. Ethical hackers conduct vishing tests to gauge employees' responses to potentially fraudulent phone calls.

9. Physical Social Engineering:

In physical social engineering, ethical hackers directly interact with employees on-site to exploit human behavior and attempt to gain unauthorized access. This technique assesses an organization's physical security and the level of awareness among employees.

In conclusion, social engineering techniques play a significant role in penetration testing, as they assess an organization's vulnerability to human-based attacks. Phishing, spear phishing, pretexting, baiting, tailgating, dumpster diving, impersonation, vishing, and physical social engineering are the primary methods used by ethical hackers to evaluate an organization's security awareness and human-based attack resilience. By conducting social engineering tests, ethical hackers provide valuable insights and recommendations to help organizations educate their employees about potential threats, enhance their security policies, and establish a robust defense against social engineering attacks. Combining technical assessments with social engineering evaluations ensures a holistic and comprehensive penetration testing approach, empowering organizations to strengthen their overall cybersecurity posture and protect sensitive information from evolving human-based threats.

CHAPTER VII
Ethical Hacking in the Real World

A. Ethical Hacking for Business and Organizations

In the rapidly evolving digital landscape, cybersecurity has become a top priority for businesses and organizations worldwide. Ethical hacking, also known as penetration testing or white-hat hacking, plays a vital role in strengthening cybersecurity defenses and safeguarding critical assets. In this section, we explore how ethical hacking is employed by businesses and organizations to proactively protect their data, networks, and reputation from cyber threats.

1. Identifying Vulnerabilities and Weaknesses:

Ethical hacking serves as a proactive approach to identifying vulnerabilities and weaknesses in an organization's systems, applications, and network infrastructure. By simulating real-world attacks, ethical hackers can pinpoint security flaws and provide detailed reports to address these issues promptly.

2. Preventing Data Breaches:

Data breaches can have severe consequences, including financial losses, reputational damage, and legal repercussions. Ethical hacking helps organizations detect and fix potential entry points before malicious actors exploit them, reducing the risk of data breaches and unauthorized access to sensitive information.

3. Ensuring Compliance with Regulations:

Many industries are subject to stringent regulations regarding data privacy and cybersecurity. Ethical hacking helps businesses ensure compliance with these regulations, such as the General Data Protection Regulation (GDPR) in the European Union or the Health Insurance Portability and Accountability Act (HIPAA) in the healthcare sector.

4. Strengthening Incident Response Preparedness:

Ethical hacking exercises, such as red teaming and penetration testing, can assess an organization's incident response capabilities. By emulating real attacks, organizations can evaluate their ability to detect, contain, and respond to security incidents effectively.

5. Enhancing Cybersecurity Awareness and Training:

Ethical hacking assessments often reveal the human factor as a significant vulnerability. By experiencing simulated phishing attacks and social engineering attempts, employees become more aware of cyber threats and are better equipped to recognize and report potential risks.

6. Third-Party Vendor Security Evaluation:

Businesses often rely on third-party vendors for various services. Ethical hacking can be used to assess the security posture of these vendors, ensuring that their practices meet the organization's cybersecurity standards and do not introduce additional risks.

7. Proactive Defense Against Emerging Threats:

The cybersecurity landscape is constantly evolving, with new threats emerging regularly. Ethical hacking allows businesses to proactively defend against evolving threats by continuously testing and improving their security measures.

8. Building Customer Trust and Reputation:

Publicized data breaches and security incidents can significantly damage an organization's reputation and erode customer trust. By investing in ethical hacking and proactive cybersecurity measures, businesses demonstrate their commitment to protecting customer data and building trust with stakeholders.

9. ROI on Cybersecurity Investments:

Investing in cybersecurity can be resource-intensive, but ethical hacking provides a substantial return on investment. The cost of recovering from a data breach or cyberattack far exceeds the cost of preventive measures, making ethical hacking a cost-effective approach to security.

In conclusion, ethical hacking is a crucial component of modern cybersecurity strategies for businesses and organizations. By identifying vulnerabilities, preventing data breaches, ensuring regulatory compliance, strengthening incident response preparedness, and enhancing cybersecurity awareness, ethical hacking contributes to a robust defense against cyber threats. Additionally, it assists in evaluating third-party vendor security, proactively defending against emerging threats, building customer trust, and achieving a significant return on cybersecurity investments. Embracing ethical hacking as an integral part of their cybersecurity initiatives empowers businesses and organizations to stay ahead of cyber adversaries and foster a secure digital environment for their operations, customers, and stakeholders.

B. Hacking Challenges in IoT and Cloud Environments

The rapid proliferation of Internet of Things (IoT) devices and the widespread adoption of cloud computing have revolutionized the way we interact with technology. While these advancements offer numerous benefits, they also introduce unique challenges in terms of cybersecurity. Ethical hacking plays a crucial role in identifying and addressing vulnerabilities in IoT and cloud environments. In this section, we explore the specific hacking challenges posed by IoT and cloud technologies and how ethical hacking helps mitigate these risks.

1. IoT Vulnerabilities and Exploitation:

The IoT ecosystem consists of a wide range of interconnected devices, from smart home appliances to industrial control systems. Many of these devices lack robust security measures, making them vulnerable to exploitation. Ethical hackers simulate attacks on IoT devices to identify weaknesses, such as default credentials, insecure communication protocols, and inadequate software updates.

2. Lack of Standardization and Patch Management:

IoT devices come from various manufacturers, leading to a lack of standardization in security practices. Moreover, patch management for IoT devices is often challenging due to limited resources or device lifespans. Ethical hacking helps uncover potential security gaps arising from patching issues and encourages manufacturers to implement secure software development practices.

3. Cloud Misconfigurations:

Cloud computing offers scalability and flexibility, but misconfigurations in cloud environments can lead to significant data exposure. Ethical hackers perform penetration testing on cloud platforms to identify misconfigured storage buckets, open ports, and overly permissive access controls, ensuring that sensitive data remains protected.

4. API Vulnerabilities:

Cloud-based services heavily rely on Application Programming Interfaces (APIs) for communication and data exchange. Vulnerabilities in APIs can expose sensitive information or allow unauthorized access. Ethical hacking focuses on testing API security and verifying that authentication, authorization, and input validation are robust.

5. Securing Edge Computing Devices:

Edge computing brings processing power closer to IoT devices, reducing latency and bandwidth requirements.

However, securing edge devices presents unique challenges as they operate in remote or physically exposed locations. Ethical hackers assess the security of edge devices, ensuring they do not serve as potential entry points for attackers.

6. Shadow IT and Cloud Service Adoption:

Shadow IT refers to unauthorized cloud service usage by employees, potentially bypassing organizational security measures. Ethical hacking evaluates the security of cloud services used within an organization, helping identify and secure unapproved cloud usage and potential risks.

7. IoT Interconnectivity Risks:

The interconnectivity of IoT devices creates a complex attack surface, where compromising one device can lead to broader network infiltration. Ethical hackers perform penetration tests on interconnected IoT systems to assess the impact of a single device compromise on the overall network security.

8. Data Privacy and Compliance:

Data privacy is critical in both IoT and cloud environments, particularly with the General Data Protection Regulation (GDPR) and other privacy regulations. Ethical hacking assesses data handling practices to ensure compliance with regulatory requirements and prevent data breaches.

In conclusion, ethical hacking plays a crucial role in addressing the unique challenges presented by IoT and cloud environments. By identifying vulnerabilities and potential risks in IoT devices, cloud configurations, APIs, and edge computing devices, ethical hackers assist organizations in developing robust security strategies. Ethical hacking helps organizations stay ahead of cyber threats, secure interconnected IoT systems, and comply with data privacy regulations. Through proactive penetration testing and vulnerability assessments, ethical hackers enable businesses and industries to harness the transformative power of IoT and cloud technologies while maintaining a resilient defense against evolving cyber risks in the real world.

C. Securing Critical Infrastructures through Ethical Hacking

Critical infrastructures, such as power grids, transportation systems, healthcare facilities, and communication networks, are the backbone of modern societies. The increasing integration of technology into these infrastructures has brought immense benefits, but it has also exposed them to significant cyber threats. Ethical hacking plays a vital role in securing critical infrastructures by proactively identifying vulnerabilities and strengthening their resilience against potential cyberattacks. In this section, we explore how ethical hacking contributes to safeguarding these essential systems.

1. Identifying Vulnerabilities in Industrial Control Systems (ICS):

Industrial control systems that manage critical infrastructures, like SCADA (Supervisory Control and Data Acquisition) systems, are susceptible to cyber threats. Ethical hackers conduct penetration tests on ICS to uncover vulnerabilities that could potentially be exploited to disrupt operations or cause physical harm.

2. Assessing Physical Security Measures:

Securing critical infrastructures goes beyond digital defenses. Ethical hackers evaluate physical security measures, such as access controls, surveillance systems, and perimeter security, to ensure unauthorized individuals cannot gain physical access to critical assets.

3. Mitigating the Impact of Cyberattacks:

By simulating cyberattacks, ethical hackers help critical infrastructure operators understand the potential consequences of a breach or cyber incident. This knowledge enables organizations to develop effective incident response plans and mitigate the impact of cyberattacks.

4. Enhancing Resilience against Nation-State Threats:

Critical infrastructures are often targeted by sophisticated nation-state actors seeking to disrupt essential services or compromise national security.

Ethical hacking strengthens defenses against such advanced threats by proactively identifying and addressing weaknesses.

5. Protecting Public Safety and Health:

Securing critical infrastructures is crucial for protecting public safety and health. Ethical hacking helps identify potential risks in healthcare facilities, emergency response systems, and transportation networks, ensuring the uninterrupted provision of essential services during emergencies.

6. Compliance with Regulatory Standards:

Many critical infrastructure sectors are subject to stringent cybersecurity regulations and standards. Ethical hacking assists organizations in complying with industry-specific guidelines and national cybersecurity frameworks.

7. Securing Smart Cities and IoT-Enabled Infrastructures:

Smart city initiatives leverage IoT technologies to optimize resource utilization and improve citizen services. Ethical hacking helps secure IoT devices, data networks, and interconnected systems to protect citizen privacy and prevent potential disruptions.

8. Developing Cybersecurity Awareness and Training Programs:

Ethical hacking supports the development of cybersecurity awareness and training programs for critical infrastructure employees. By conducting phishing simulations and social engineering tests, ethical hackers educate personnel about cyber threats and the importance of following security protocols.

9. Strengthening Public-Private Partnerships:

Securing critical infrastructures requires collaboration between public and private sectors. Ethical hackers facilitate this cooperation by engaging with government agencies, infrastructure operators, and cybersecurity firms to share best practices and threat intelligence.

In conclusion, critical infrastructures are high-value targets for cyber adversaries, making their security of paramount importance. Ethical hacking serves as a proactive and strategic approach to identify vulnerabilities, assess physical and digital security measures, and enhance resilience against cyber threats. By securing industrial control systems, mitigating the impact of cyberattacks, and protecting public safety, ethical hacking plays a vital role in safeguarding the functioning and continuity of critical infrastructures. Additionally, compliance with regulatory standards, securing smart cities and IoT-enabled infrastructures, and developing cybersecurity awareness programs further strengthen the resilience of these essential systems. Ethical hackers' efforts not only protect critical infrastructures but also contribute to the overall safety, stability, and prosperity of nations in the face of evolving cyber threats in the real world.

CHAPTER VIII
Advanced Ethical Hacking Concepts

A. Evading Intrusion Detection Systems (IDS) and Firewalls

As cybersecurity defenses become more sophisticated, ethical hackers must continually evolve their techniques to stay ahead in the cat-and-mouse game with security systems. Intrusion Detection Systems (IDS) and firewalls are crucial components of network security, designed to detect and prevent unauthorized access and malicious activities. In this section, we explore the advanced techniques ethical hackers use to evade IDS and firewalls while conducting penetration testing.

1. Polymorphic Malware:

Polymorphic malware is a type of malicious software that can change its code and appearance to evade signature-based detection employed by IDS and antivirus solutions. Ethical hackers utilize polymorphic malware to test the effectiveness of an organization's security infrastructure in detecting new and evolving threats.

2. Encrypted Communication:

Traditional IDS and firewalls may have difficulty inspecting encrypted traffic. Ethical hackers leverage encrypted communication channels, such as Virtual Private Networks (VPNs) or encrypted protocols, to bypass security controls and remain undetected during their penetration tests.

3. Traffic Fragmentation:

Splitting network traffic into smaller fragments can be used to evade IDS and firewalls that rely on analyzing complete packets. Ethical hackers may use fragmentation techniques to send malicious payloads in a manner that goes undetected by security systems.

4. Protocol Tunneling:

Protocol tunneling involves encapsulating one protocol within another. Ethical hackers can tunnel malicious traffic within legitimate protocols, evading signature-based detection and firewall rules that may not be aware of the hidden payload.

5. IP Spoofing:

IP spoofing is a technique where an attacker alters the source IP address of network packets to appear as if they originate from a trusted source. Ethical hackers may employ IP spoofing to bypass access controls and trick IDS and firewalls into allowing unauthorized traffic.

6. Session Hijacking:

Session hijacking involves taking control of an authenticated user's session to gain unauthorized access to a system. Ethical hackers can attempt to hijack sessions and evade detection by impersonating legitimate users with authorized access.

7. Covert Channels:

Covert channels are hidden communication paths that allow data to be exchanged between entities in a manner that may not be detected by IDS or firewalls. Ethical hackers may use covert channels to evade network monitoring and extract data discreetly.

8. Zero-Day Exploits:

Zero-day exploits target newly discovered vulnerabilities that are not yet patched or known to security vendors. Ethical hackers can use zero-day exploits to bypass security controls that are not prepared to detect or prevent such attacks.

9. Behavior-Based Evasion:

Ethical hackers can modify their attack patterns and behaviors to evade behavior-based detection mechanisms employed by IDS and firewalls. By adjusting attack timings, sequencing, and payload delivery, ethical hackers make it more challenging for security systems to recognize their malicious activities.

In conclusion, evading Intrusion Detection Systems (IDS) and firewalls represents a significant challenge for ethical hackers during penetration testing. Polymorphic malware, encrypted communication, traffic fragmentation, protocol tunneling, IP spoofing, session hijacking, covert channels, zero-day exploits, and behavior-based evasion are advanced techniques used by ethical hackers to assess the effectiveness of an organization's security measures. By employing these evasion techniques responsibly, ethical hackers help organizations identify weaknesses in their defense strategies, improve incident response capabilities, and stay resilient against evolving cyber threats. The knowledge gained from ethical hacking assessments allows organizations to fine-tune their security controls, update their threat detection capabilities, and proactively protect their digital assets in a constantly evolving cybersecurity landscape.

B. Advanced Persistent Threats (APTs) and Countermeasures

Advanced Persistent Threats (APTs) are sophisticated and stealthy cyberattacks launched by highly skilled adversaries with specific objectives. APTs aim to infiltrate and remain undetected within a target network for an extended period, allowing attackers to access sensitive data, steal intellectual property, or conduct espionage. Ethical hackers play a crucial role in understanding APT techniques and developing countermeasures to defend against these persistent threats. In this section, we explore APTs and the countermeasures employed by ethical hackers to protect organizations.

1. APT Characteristics:

APTs are characterized by their long-term and targeted nature. They often employ multiple attack vectors, such as spear-phishing, social engineering, and zero-day exploits, to gain initial access. Once inside the network, APTs utilize advanced tactics to remain hidden, including lateral movement, privilege escalation, and encryption of command and control traffic.

2. Threat Intelligence Gathering:

Ethical hackers actively gather threat intelligence to understand the tactics, techniques, and procedures (TTPs) used by APT groups. By analyzing APT behavior and historical data, they can identify patterns and indicators of compromise that help organizations detect and respond to APT activities.

3. Continuous Monitoring and Detection:

To detect APTs, organizations must adopt a proactive approach to security. Ethical hackers implement continuous monitoring and advanced threat detection tools to identify suspicious activities, anomalous behaviors, and potential APT activity in real-time.

4. Endpoint Detection and Response (EDR):

Endpoint Detection and Response solutions help organizations monitor and respond to suspicious activities on individual devices. Ethical hackers deploy EDR tools to detect APTs operating within an organization's endpoints and promptly respond to potential threats.

5. Network Segmentation:

Network segmentation is a critical defensive strategy to limit lateral movement within the network. Ethical hackers advocate for implementing strong network segmentation to contain APTs and prevent attackers from moving laterally and accessing sensitive data.

6. Deception Technologies:

Deception technologies involve deploying fake assets or "honeypots" within the network to deceive attackers and divert their attention from real targets. Ethical hackers utilize deception techniques to detect and engage with APTs, gathering valuable insights on their behavior and intentions.

7. Incident Response Planning:

Ethical hackers assist organizations in developing comprehensive incident response plans tailored to APT scenarios. These plans outline the steps to be taken in the event of an APT breach, enabling a swift and coordinated response to mitigate the impact.

8. Threat Hunting:

Threat hunting is a proactive approach to search for APTs and other hidden threats within the network. Ethical hackers conduct threat hunting exercises to actively seek out potential APT indicators and eliminate them before they cause significant harm.

9. Employee Training and Awareness:

Human error remains a significant factor in APT success. Ethical hackers advocate for regular employee training and awareness programs to educate personnel about APT risks, phishing attacks, and social engineering tactics, empowering them to recognize and report potential threats.

In conclusion, Advanced Persistent Threats (APTs) represent a formidable challenge for organizations due to their persistence and sophistication. Ethical hackers play a crucial role in combating APTs by understanding their characteristics, gathering threat intelligence, and developing effective countermeasures. Continuous monitoring, network segmentation, deception technologies, incident response planning, and threat hunting are essential components of APT defense strategies. Additionally, employee training and awareness programs are vital in building a resilient human firewall against APT-related social engineering attacks. By adopting proactive defense measures and leveraging the expertise of ethical hackers, organizations can enhance their cybersecurity posture and better protect themselves against the evolving threat landscape of Advanced Persistent Threats.

C. Reverse Engineering and Exploit Development

Reverse engineering and exploit development are two advanced ethical hacking concepts that enable cybersecurity professionals to understand the inner workings of software, identify vulnerabilities, and create effective exploits. These skills are essential for ethical hackers as they seek to responsibly identify and address weaknesses in software and systems. In this section, we delve into the significance of reverse engineering and exploit development in ethical hacking practices.

1. Reverse Engineering:

Reverse engineering involves the process of analyzing a software program or binary to understand its functionality, structure, and behavior. Ethical hackers use reverse engineering to examine proprietary software or malware, identify potential security flaws, and devise effective countermeasures. Reverse engineering can also help in understanding undocumented protocols and APIs, enabling the creation of compatible software or enhancing security controls.

2. Disassembly and Decompilation:

Disassembly is the process of converting machine code (binary) into assembly language to comprehend the program's low-level instructions. Decompilation involves converting compiled code back into a higher-level language like C or C++. Ethical hackers use disassembly and decompilation techniques to gain insights into the software's logic and algorithms.

3. Identifying Vulnerabilities:

Through reverse engineering, ethical hackers can identify vulnerabilities such as buffer overflows, memory corruption, and injection flaws that could potentially be exploited by malicious actors. Understanding these vulnerabilities helps in responsibly disclosing them to software vendors for timely patching.

4. Patch Analysis:

Reverse engineering is instrumental in analyzing software patches released by vendors to fix vulnerabilities. Ethical hackers can study patch details to infer the nature of the underlying vulnerability and assess its severity.

5. Exploit Development:

Exploit development involves creating software exploits that leverage identified vulnerabilities to gain unauthorized access or execute malicious code. Ethical hackers utilize exploit development skills to validate vulnerabilities and demonstrate their impact, which helps organizations understand the potential consequences of unpatched flaws.

6. Responsible Disclosure:

Ethical hackers play a crucial role in responsibly disclosing vulnerabilities they discover through reverse engineering and exploit development. By adhering to established disclosure procedures, they collaborate with software vendors to address the identified issues before malicious actors can exploit them.

7. Zero-Day Exploits:

Zero-day exploits are attacks targeting newly discovered vulnerabilities before vendors have had a chance to release patches. Ethical hackers may develop proof-of-concept (PoC) zero-day exploits to illustrate the severity of the vulnerability and motivate prompt patching.

8. Secure Software Development:

Reverse engineering provides valuable insights into the security weaknesses of software. Ethical hackers use this knowledge to advocate for secure software development practices, encouraging developers to write code with fewer vulnerabilities and robust security controls.

9. Malware Analysis:

Reverse engineering is a fundamental aspect of malware analysis. Ethical hackers dissect malware to understand its capabilities, infection vectors, and potential impact on systems. This knowledge aids in creating effective malware detection and removal tools.

In conclusion, reverse engineering and exploit development are indispensable skills for ethical hackers in their mission to identify and address software vulnerabilities responsibly. By reverse engineering software, ethical hackers gain insights into its inner workings and uncover potential weaknesses. This knowledge is crucial for identifying vulnerabilities, understanding the impact of patches, and promoting secure software development practices. Additionally, exploit development enables ethical hackers to create proofs-of-concept and validate the severity of identified vulnerabilities, aiding in responsible disclosure and timely patching. Reverse engineering also plays a vital role in malware analysis, helping ethical hackers understand and combat the ever-evolving threats posed by malicious software. Through these advanced concepts, ethical hackers enhance their capabilities and contribute significantly to the proactive defense of organizations and the broader cybersecurity landscape.

CHAPTER IX
Ethical Hacking for Defense

A. Implementing Effective Cybersecurity Measures

In an era of constant cyber threats, implementing effective cybersecurity measures is imperative for organizations to protect their sensitive data, critical assets, and reputation. Ethical hacking plays a vital role in this regard, as it helps identify vulnerabilities before malicious actors can exploit them. In this section, we explore the key components of implementing robust cybersecurity measures with the aid of ethical hacking practices.

1. Vulnerability Assessments and Penetration Testing:

Vulnerability assessments and penetration testing are essential components of a proactive cybersecurity strategy. Ethical hackers conduct these assessments to identify weaknesses in an organization's systems, applications, and networks. By simulating real-world attacks, ethical hackers provide insights into potential entry points and security gaps, enabling organizations to remediate vulnerabilities before attackers can exploit them.

2. Secure Network Architecture:

Implementing a secure network architecture is critical for defending against cyber threats. Ethical hackers help organizations design and deploy networks with strong segmentation, firewall rules, access controls, and intrusion detection systems. A well-architected network can prevent lateral movement by attackers and limit the impact of potential breaches.

3. Patch Management and Updates:

Keeping software, operating systems, and applications up to date is crucial to address known vulnerabilities. Ethical hackers emphasize the importance of regular patch management and updates to minimize the risk of exploitation through outdated or unpatched software.

4. Security Awareness Training:

Human error remains a significant factor in cyber incidents. Ethical hackers advocate for comprehensive security awareness training programs to educate employees about cyber threats, phishing attacks, and social engineering tactics. Well-informed employees are more likely to recognize and report potential security risks.

5. Incident Response Planning:

Having a well-defined incident response plan is essential for swift and effective handling of cyber incidents. Ethical hackers assist organizations in developing incident response procedures, outlining roles and responsibilities, and conducting tabletop exercises to test the response plan's effectiveness.

6. Encryption and Data Protection:

Data encryption is critical for safeguarding sensitive information from unauthorized access. Ethical hackers advise organizations to implement robust encryption protocols for data at rest and in transit, ensuring that even if a breach occurs, the stolen data remains encrypted and unusable to attackers.

7. Access Controls and Privilege Management:

Limiting access to sensitive data and systems is vital for minimizing the impact of a potential breach. Ethical hackers recommend implementing least privilege principles, ensuring that employees have access only to the resources necessary for their roles.

8. Continuous Monitoring and Threat Detection:

Ethical hackers emphasize the importance of continuous monitoring and threat detection tools. Implementing security solutions that can detect anomalous behavior and potential threats in real-time enables organizations to respond proactively to emerging cyber incidents.

9. Third-Party Security Assessments:

Many organizations rely on third-party vendors for various services. Ethical hackers recommend conducting security assessments of third-party vendors to ensure they meet the organization's cybersecurity standards and do not introduce additional risks.

In conclusion, ethical hacking plays a pivotal role in implementing effective cybersecurity measures for organizations. Vulnerability assessments, penetration testing, secure network architecture, patch management, security awareness training, incident response planning, encryption, access controls, continuous monitoring, and third-party security assessments are critical components of a robust defense strategy. By leveraging ethical hacking practices, organizations can identify and remediate vulnerabilities, enhance their overall cybersecurity posture, and build a proactive defense against cyber threats. With the aid of ethical hackers, organizations are better equipped to stay ahead of cyber adversaries and safeguard their valuable assets in an ever-evolving cybersecurity landscape.

B. Incident Response and Handling

In the ever-evolving landscape of cyber threats, organizations must be prepared to respond swiftly and effectively to security incidents. Incident response and handling is a crucial aspect of cybersecurity defense, enabling organizations to detect, contain, eradicate, and recover from cyberattacks. Ethical hacking plays a significant role in incident response by helping organizations proactively identify weaknesses and improve their response capabilities. In this section, we delve into the importance of incident response and how ethical hacking enhances an organization's ability to handle security incidents.

1. Proactive Incident Response Planning:

Ethical hackers work closely with organizations to develop proactive incident response plans tailored to their specific needs and risk profiles. Incident response planning involves defining roles and responsibilities, establishing communication protocols, and creating a step-by-step guide to handle different types of security incidents effectively.

2. Detecting and Responding to Intrusions:

Ethical hackers conduct regular security assessments, vulnerability scanning, and penetration testing to detect potential intrusions or suspicious activities within an organization's network. By identifying security weaknesses, organizations can respond promptly to potential threats and mitigate their impact.

3. Incident Containment and Eradication:

When an incident occurs, swift and decisive action is essential to contain the threat and prevent further damage. Ethical hackers assist in isolating affected systems, removing malware, and eradicating the attacker's presence from the network.

4. Forensic Analysis and Evidence Preservation:

Effective incident response involves conducting forensic analysis to understand the scope and impact of the breach. Ethical hackers follow best practices in evidence preservation to ensure that critical digital evidence is intact and usable in potential legal proceedings.

5. Communication and Coordination:

Incident response often requires seamless communication and coordination among different teams, such as IT, security, legal, and management.

Ethical hackers help organizations establish clear lines of communication and define roles to ensure a well-coordinated incident response effort.

6. Post-Incident Recovery:

After containing the incident, ethical hackers aid in post-incident recovery efforts. This involves restoring affected systems, validating data integrity, and implementing additional security measures to prevent similar incidents in the future.

7. Continuous Improvement and Lessons Learned:

Ethical hacking contributes to continuous improvement in incident response capabilities. By analyzing incidents and identifying areas for improvement, organizations can refine their incident response plans and enhance their ability to handle future security incidents effectively.

8. Red Team Exercises:

Red team exercises, conducted by ethical hackers, simulate real-world attacks to test an organization's incident response capabilities under realistic conditions.

These exercises identify gaps in the response process and provide valuable insights for refining incident response plans.

9. Collaborating with External Stakeholders:

Incident response often involves collaboration with external stakeholders, such as law enforcement, industry peers, and regulatory bodies. Ethical hackers assist organizations in establishing these collaborative relationships to ensure a coordinated and comprehensive response to security incidents.

In conclusion, incident response and handling are critical components of a robust cybersecurity defense strategy. Ethical hacking plays a pivotal role in incident response by proactively identifying vulnerabilities, enabling swift incident detection, containing and eradicating threats, and aiding in post-incident recovery. By working closely with organizations to develop incident response plans, conducting red team exercises, and collaborating with external stakeholders, ethical hackers help organizations strengthen their incident response capabilities and effectively protect their assets and data. In an era of sophisticated cyber threats, organizations must embrace the expertise of ethical hackers to build resilient incident response processes that ensure minimal damage and downtime in the face of security incidents.

C. Security Awareness and Training for Users

As the human element remains a significant factor in cyber incidents, security awareness and training for users are critical components of a robust cybersecurity defense strategy. Ethical hacking advocates for empowering employees with the knowledge and skills to recognize and respond to cyber threats effectively. In this section, we explore the importance of security awareness and training for users and how ethical hacking plays a pivotal role in promoting a security-conscious culture within organizations.

1. Understanding Cyber Threats:

Ethical hacking emphasizes the need for employees to understand various cyber threats, including phishing, social engineering, ransomware, and malware attacks. Through interactive training sessions and real-world examples, employees learn to recognize suspicious activities and potential red flags.

2. Recognizing Phishing Attempts:

Phishing remains one of the most prevalent attack vectors used by cybercriminals. Ethical hacking includes phishing simulation exercises to train employees in identifying phishing emails and websites. By practicing safe email habits and not clicking on suspicious links, employees become the first line of defense against phishing attacks.

3. Social Engineering Awareness:

Social engineering tactics often exploit human emotions and behaviors to manipulate individuals into divulging sensitive information or performing unauthorized actions. Ethical hackers educate employees about social engineering techniques, such as pretexting and baiting, to foster a sense of caution when interacting with unknown individuals or unsolicited requests.

4. Password Management:

Ethical hacking emphasizes the importance of strong password management practices. Employees are trained to create complex passwords, avoid password reuse, and utilize multi-factor authentication to add an extra layer of security to their accounts.

5. Safe Internet and Device Usage:

Ethical hacking includes training on safe internet browsing and the responsible use of personal devices for work-related purposes. Employees learn to identify potentially unsafe websites and understand the risks associated with connecting to unsecured Wi-Fi networks.

6. Reporting Security Incidents:

Creating a culture where employees feel comfortable reporting security incidents is crucial. Ethical hacking promotes an open reporting culture, where employees are encouraged to promptly report suspicious activities or potential security breaches to the appropriate personnel.

7. Mobile Security Best Practices:

With the increasing use of mobile devices, ethical hacking emphasizes mobile security best practices. Employees learn about secure app downloads, regular software updates, and the importance of protecting their mobile devices with passwords or biometric authentication.

8. Data Protection and Privacy Awareness:

Employees are educated on the significance of data protection and privacy. Ethical hackers stress the importance of handling sensitive information responsibly and complying with data protection regulations to prevent data breaches and privacy violations.

9. Continuous Learning and Updates:

Cyber threats evolve rapidly, and security awareness training must keep pace. Ethical hacking advocates for continuous learning and updates to ensure employees stay informed about emerging threats and security best practices.

In conclusion, security awareness and training for users are fundamental elements of a strong cybersecurity defense. Ethical hacking recognizes that employees are both potential targets and the first line of defense against cyber threats. By empowering employees with knowledge about various cyber threats, phishing attempts, social engineering techniques, and safe internet and device usage, organizations create a security-conscious workforce capable of identifying and responding to potential risks. Reporting security incidents, following password management best practices, and understanding data protection and privacy principles further enhance an organization's cybersecurity posture. Ethical hacking fosters a culture of continuous learning, ensuring that security awareness training remains relevant and effective in the face of evolving cyber threats. Ultimately, a well-informed and security-aware workforce is an organization's greatest asset in mitigating cyber risks and safeguarding valuable assets and data.

CHAPTER X
The Future of Ethical Hacking

A. Emerging Trends and Technologies in Ethical Hacking

Ethical hacking, as a crucial component of cybersecurity defense, continues to evolve in response to the ever-changing cyber threat landscape. As new technologies emerge, ethical hackers must adapt their skills and techniques to stay ahead of malicious actors. In this section, we explore the emerging trends and technologies in ethical hacking that will shape the future of cybersecurity.

1. Artificial Intelligence (AI) and Machine Learning (ML) in Ethical Hacking:

AI and ML are transforming various industries, and ethical hacking is no exception. Ethical hackers are exploring the use of AI and ML to automate vulnerability scanning, detect anomalies, and improve threat detection and response capabilities. These technologies enable faster and more efficient identification of potential risks and cyber threats.

2. IoT Security Challenges:

The Internet of Things (IoT) presents unique security challenges due to the proliferation of interconnected devices. Ethical hackers are increasingly focusing on identifying vulnerabilities in IoT devices and advocating for security-by-design principles to ensure the safety and privacy of IoT users.

3. Cloud Security:

As organizations transition to cloud-based services, cloud security becomes a top priority. Ethical hackers are developing expertise in cloud security assessment, helping organizations identify misconfigurations, data exposures, and other cloud-related risks.

4. Blockchain Security:

Blockchain technology offers decentralized and secure data storage. However, its implementation is not immune to security risks. Ethical hackers are exploring blockchain security to identify potential vulnerabilities and ensure the integrity and immutability of blockchain-based systems.

5. Quantum Computing and Cryptography:

The advent of quantum computing poses both opportunities and challenges for cybersecurity. Ethical hackers are researching quantum-safe cryptography to protect sensitive information from potential quantum-based attacks in the future.

6. Bug Bounty Programs:

Bug bounty programs are becoming increasingly popular, with organizations incentivizing ethical hackers to discover and responsibly disclose vulnerabilities in their systems. Ethical hackers play a vital role in these programs, helping organizations fortify their defenses by providing real-world feedback.

7. Cyber Range Training:

Cyber range training environments simulate real-world cyberattacks and scenarios, enabling ethical hackers to practice their skills in a controlled setting. Cyber range training helps ethical hackers stay sharp and develop practical experience in handling sophisticated cyber threats.

8. Red Team and Purple Team Exercises:

Red team exercises simulate adversarial attacks, while purple team exercises involve collaboration between red and blue teams to assess and improve an organization's defensive capabilities. These exercises provide valuable insights into an organization's security strengths and weaknesses.

9. Automated Exploitation Tools:

Ethical hackers are leveraging automated exploitation tools to streamline the process of identifying and validating vulnerabilities. These tools enable ethical hackers to assess a large number of systems efficiently and focus on complex exploitation techniques.

In conclusion, the future of ethical hacking is marked by continuous advancements in technologies and methodologies to address emerging cyber threats. AI and ML are transforming ethical hacking by enhancing threat detection and response capabilities. The rise of IoT, cloud, and blockchain technologies introduces new security challenges, prompting ethical hackers to develop specialized skills to protect these systems. Quantum computing and cryptography present a need for quantum-safe solutions to safeguard data against future threats. Bug bounty programs incentivize ethical hackers to contribute actively to cybersecurity defense. Cyber range training, red team, and purple team exercises foster continuous skill development and improve incident response capabilities. The automation of exploitation tools streamlines vulnerability assessment processes, allowing ethical hackers to focus on high-impact areas. As the cyber landscape continues to evolve, ethical hacking will remain an essential pillar of cybersecurity defense, and ethical hackers will play a vital role in safeguarding digital assets and data from malicious actors in the dynamic and interconnected world of tomorrow.

B. Ethical Hacking's Role in Shaping Cybersecurity Policies

As the world becomes increasingly interconnected and reliant on technology, the importance of strong cybersecurity policies cannot be overstated. Ethical hacking plays a significant role in shaping these policies by providing valuable insights, identifying vulnerabilities, and advocating for security best practices. In this section, we explore how ethical hacking influences the development and implementation of cybersecurity policies to create a safer digital landscape.

1. Identifying Vulnerabilities and Weaknesses:

Ethical hackers conduct rigorous security assessments, including penetration testing and vulnerability assessments, to identify weaknesses in organizations' networks, applications, and systems. By uncovering potential entry points for cybercriminals, ethical hackers highlight areas that need attention, helping policymakers focus on critical cybersecurity issues.

2. Real-World Threat Simulations:

Ethical hacking involves conducting realistic threat simulations and red team exercises that imitate actual cyberattacks. These simulations provide policymakers with a firsthand understanding of potential risks and their impact. Policymakers can use this knowledge to develop comprehensive strategies that address current and emerging cyber threats effectively.

3. Proactive Defense Strategies:

Ethical hackers emphasize the importance of a proactive defense approach in cybersecurity policies. Instead of solely reacting to cyber incidents, ethical hacking advocates for continuous monitoring, regular security assessments, and threat hunting to detect and mitigate threats before they escalate.

4. Encouraging Responsible Vulnerability Disclosure:

Ethical hackers promote responsible vulnerability disclosure practices. Policymakers work alongside ethical hackers to create frameworks that encourage responsible disclosure of vulnerabilities to relevant organizations, allowing for timely patching and mitigation.

5. Collaborating with Government and Industry:

Ethical hackers collaborate with government agencies, regulatory bodies, and industry peers to share threat intelligence and best practices. Policymakers leverage these collaborations to gain valuable insights into emerging cyber threats, industry trends, and effective cybersecurity measures.

6. Raising Awareness about Cyber Risks:

Ethical hacking plays a critical role in raising awareness among policymakers and the general public about the severity of cyber risks. By demonstrating the potential consequences of cyberattacks, ethical hackers help policymakers understand the urgency of implementing robust cybersecurity policies.

7. Evaluating Privacy and Data Protection Measures:

Ethical hackers assess the effectiveness of privacy and data protection measures in various systems. This evaluation assists policymakers in developing and updating data protection laws and regulations, ensuring that individuals' sensitive information is safeguarded.

8. Promoting Cybersecurity Education:

Ethical hackers advocate for cybersecurity education initiatives at all levels, from schools to the workplace. Policymakers recognize the importance of building a cybersecurity-aware culture and invest in educational programs to empower individuals with the knowledge and skills to protect themselves and their organizations.

9. Encouraging Cybersecurity Compliance and Standards:

Ethical hacking reinforces the importance of complying with cybersecurity standards and industry best practices. Policymakers use these insights to create and enforce cybersecurity regulations that promote a high standard of security across industries.

In conclusion, ethical hacking plays a vital role in shaping cybersecurity policies that are responsive, proactive, and effective in safeguarding the digital landscape. By identifying vulnerabilities, conducting real-world threat simulations, and advocating for responsible disclosure and proactive defense strategies, ethical hackers provide critical inputs for policymakers to develop comprehensive cybersecurity policies. Collaboration with government agencies, industry peers, and educational institutions enables policymakers to stay informed about emerging cyber threats and industry trends. Ethical hacking's contribution in evaluating data protection measures, raising awareness about cyber risks, and promoting cybersecurity education fosters a security-conscious culture within society. Ultimately, ethical hacking's role in shaping cybersecurity policies strengthens the collective defense against cyber threats and fosters a safer and more resilient digital future for individuals, organizations, and nations alike.

C. Ethical Hacking as a Career and Its Future Prospects

Ethical hacking has emerged as a rewarding and in-demand career path in the field of cybersecurity. As organizations worldwide recognize the critical need for robust cybersecurity defenses, ethical hackers play a vital role in safeguarding digital assets and data. In this section, we explore the prospects of ethical hacking as a career and how it is poised for significant growth in the future.

1. Increasing Demand for Cybersecurity Experts:

With the rise in cyber threats and high-profile data breaches, the demand for skilled cybersecurity professionals, including ethical hackers, continues to soar. Organizations across industries seek experts who can identify vulnerabilities, conduct penetration testing, and enhance their overall security posture.

2. Variety of Career Paths:

Ethical hacking offers a wide range of career paths and specializations. From penetration testers and vulnerability analysts to security consultants and incident response experts, ethical hackers can choose from diverse roles that align with their interests and expertise.

3. Continuous Skill Development:

The dynamic nature of cybersecurity requires ethical hackers to stay updated with the latest trends, technologies, and threats. As a result, ethical hacking as a career encourages continuous skill development, learning, and staying abreast of emerging tools and techniques.

4. Advancements in Technology:

The future of ethical hacking is closely intertwined with technological advancements. As new technologies emerge, ethical hackers will need to adapt their skills to assess and secure IoT devices, cloud-based systems, blockchain, and AI-powered applications.

5. Expanding Scope of Ethical Hacking:

The scope of ethical hacking extends beyond traditional IT systems. Ethical hackers will increasingly play a significant role in securing critical infrastructures, medical devices, autonomous vehicles, and other emerging technologies.

6. Ethical Hacking in Government and Defense:

Governments and defense organizations are recognizing the importance of ethical hacking to protect their critical assets and national security. Ethical hackers will find opportunities in governmental agencies and defense industries to contribute to national cybersecurity efforts.

7. Remote and Global Opportunities:

Ethical hacking allows professionals to work remotely and collaborate with teams worldwide. The global nature of cyber threats means that ethical hackers can provide services and support to organizations regardless of their geographic location.

8. Bug Bounty Programs and Freelancing:

Bug bounty programs hosted by various companies and organizations provide ethical hackers with opportunities to earn rewards by identifying and responsibly disclosing vulnerabilities. Additionally, ethical hackers can work as freelancers, offering their services to multiple clients and projects.

9. Certifications and Professional Development:

Ethical hacking certifications, such as Certified Ethical Hacker (CEH) and Offensive Security Certified Professional (OSCP), are recognized and valued by employers. Ethical hackers can enhance their career prospects by obtaining relevant certifications and engaging in professional development activities.

In conclusion, ethical hacking offers a promising and rewarding career path with a bright future ahead. The increasing demand for cybersecurity experts, continuous skill development, expanding scope, and global opportunities make ethical hacking an attractive profession for cybersecurity enthusiasts. As technology advances and cyber threats evolve, ethical hackers will remain at the forefront of protecting organizations and individuals from malicious actors. Ethical hacking as a career path offers diverse roles and specializations, allowing professionals to align their passion with their work. With the critical role ethical hackers play in securing digital assets, governments, defense organizations, and businesses worldwide will continue to invest in cybersecurity talent.

CHAPTER XI
Ethical Hacking Challenges and Ethics in the Evolving Digital Landscape

A. The Global Ethical Hacking Community

In the ever-evolving digital landscape, the global ethical hacking community plays a crucial role in safeguarding digital assets and promoting cybersecurity best practices. Ethical hackers, also known as white hat hackers, are cybersecurity professionals who use their skills for good, identifying vulnerabilities and assisting organizations in fortifying their defenses. In this section, we explore the challenges and ethics faced by the global ethical hacking community as they navigate the complex and dynamic world of cybersecurity.

1. Legal and Regulatory Challenges:

Ethical hackers often operate in a legal gray area, and their actions may raise legal and regulatory concerns. While their intentions are altruistic, their activities could be misconstrued or inadvertently cross boundaries. Ethical hackers must carefully adhere to laws and regulations related to cybersecurity and responsible disclosure to avoid potential legal repercussions.

2. Responsible Disclosure Dilemmas:

One of the ethical challenges faced by the global ethical hacking community is responsible disclosure. While identifying vulnerabilities is essential, deciding when and how to disclose them can be a delicate balance. Ethical hackers must consider the impact of their findings on an organization's reputation and security, as well as the potential risks posed by malicious actors if the vulnerability is made public before a patch is available.

3. Vulnerability Stockpiling and Zero-Days:

Some ethical hackers discover critical vulnerabilities, but due to various reasons, the vulnerabilities may not be promptly disclosed or patched. This situation leads to vulnerability stockpiling and the emergence of zero-day exploits. Ethical hackers must weigh the implications of holding onto such information and the potential harm it can cause if it falls into the wrong hands.

4. Conflicts with Bug Bounty Programs:

While bug bounty programs offer incentives for responsible vulnerability disclosure, ethical hackers might face conflicts when a company does not recognize the severity of a discovered vulnerability or refuses to provide a fair reward. Balancing the responsibility to secure systems with financial compensation can be a challenge for ethical hackers.

5. Collaborative Threat Intelligence Sharing:

Ethical hackers recognize the importance of sharing threat intelligence to strengthen cybersecurity defenses collectively. However, not all organizations are open to sharing data due to concerns about proprietary information or reputational risks. The ethical hacking community faces challenges in fostering a culture of open and collaborative threat intelligence sharing.

6. Ethics in Offensive Security:

As ethical hackers explore offensive security techniques, such as social engineering and physical penetration testing, ethical concerns may arise. Ethical hackers must ensure that their actions are conducted with clear authorization and do not cause harm to individuals or organizations.

7. Transparency and Accountability:

Ethical hackers are entrusted with significant responsibilities in the cybersecurity domain. Maintaining transparency in their actions and being accountable for the consequences of their findings are essential aspects of their ethical conduct.

8. Professionalism and Integrity:

The global ethical hacking community upholds professionalism and integrity in their interactions with clients, fellow professionals, and the broader cybersecurity ecosystem. Upholding ethical standards and maintaining trust are paramount for the community's credibility.

In conclusion, the global ethical hacking community faces various challenges and ethical considerations in their mission to protect the digital landscape. Legal and regulatory concerns, responsible disclosure dilemmas, vulnerability stockpiling, and conflicts with bug bounty programs are some of the complex issues that ethical hackers navigate. Collaborative threat intelligence sharing and ethics in offensive security further shape the ethical hacking landscape. Transparency, accountability, professionalism, and integrity are foundational principles that guide ethical hackers in their endeavors. As the cybersecurity landscape continues to evolve, the global ethical hacking community must address these challenges and uphold ethical standards to ensure a safer digital world. By adhering to ethical principles, ethical hackers play a vital role in promoting cybersecurity resilience and enhancing trust in the digital ecosystem.

B. Addressing New Ethical Dilemmas in Ethical Hacking

As the digital landscape evolves, ethical hacking faces new challenges and ethical dilemmas that require careful consideration and adaptation. Ethical hackers are at the forefront of defending against cyber threats, but the complex nature of cybersecurity presents novel ethical concerns. In this section, we explore some of the new ethical dilemmas in ethical hacking and the approaches to address them responsibly.

1. AI and Automation in Ethical Hacking:

The increasing use of artificial intelligence (AI) and automation in cybersecurity raises ethical questions. Ethical hackers must assess how these technologies impact their work, including ethical implications related to the use of AI for offensive security or autonomous decision-making in vulnerability assessments. Striking a balance between human judgment and AI-driven processes is crucial to ensure ethical conduct.

2. Ethical Hacking in Nation-State Contexts:

Ethical hacking can take place in the context of nation-state cybersecurity efforts. Ethical hackers may be engaged in offensive activities to protect national security. However, this raises ethical concerns about potential collateral damage, privacy violations, and adherence to international norms. Ethical hackers operating in such contexts must be mindful of their responsibilities and the broader implications of their actions.

3. Deepfakes and Cyber Misinformation:

The rise of deepfake technology presents ethical dilemmas in the domain of cybersecurity. Ethical hackers must consider the implications of using deepfake techniques for defensive or offensive purposes, as these technologies can blur the lines between truth and misinformation. The responsible use of deepfake technology is vital to maintain ethical standards.

4. Dual-Use Technologies:

Certain hacking tools and techniques have dual-use capabilities, meaning they can be used for both ethical and malicious purposes. Ethical hackers must critically assess the potential risks and benefits of using such tools and avoid contributing to the proliferation of offensive capabilities in the wrong hands.

5. Cybersecurity for Human Rights:

Ethical hacking intersects with human rights concerns when it comes to issues like surveillance, privacy, and digital freedom. Ethical hackers must consider the impact of their actions on individuals' rights and freedoms and avoid contributing to human rights abuses or privacy violations.

6. Bias and Fairness in Cybersecurity Algorithms:

AI-driven cybersecurity algorithms can be susceptible to bias, which may lead to unfair treatment or discrimination against certain groups. Ethical hackers must be vigilant in ensuring that the algorithms they develop or employ do not perpetuate biases or exacerbate existing social inequalities.

7. Environmental Impact of Cybersecurity Practices:

Cybersecurity practices, particularly those involving extensive computing resources, can have environmental consequences. Ethical hackers must consider the environmental impact of their work and strive for sustainable and energy-efficient approaches.

8. Balancing Disclosure and Security:

Ethical hackers often discover vulnerabilities that could have significant consequences if exploited. Striking the right balance between timely disclosure and maintaining security until a patch is available is a delicate ethical dilemma. Responsible disclosure practices are crucial to minimize harm while ensuring that vulnerabilities are addressed.

In conclusion, as ethical hacking navigates the evolving digital landscape, new ethical dilemmas arise that demand thoughtful consideration and ethical decision-making. The adoption of AI and automation, ethical hacking in nation-state contexts, deepfakes and cyber misinformation, dual-use technologies, cybersecurity for human rights, fairness in algorithms, environmental impact, and responsible disclosure all present unique challenges that ethical hackers must address. Ethical hackers play a vital role in shaping the ethical framework of cybersecurity practices, ensuring that their actions align with responsible conduct and adhere to ethical standards. By being vigilant and proactive in addressing these ethical dilemmas, ethical hackers can uphold their commitment to protect digital assets and privacy while contributing to a safer and more secure digital world for everyone.

C. Striking the Balance between Privacy and Security

In the dynamic and ever-evolving digital landscape, the ethical hacking community faces a significant challenge in striking the delicate balance between privacy and security. While the primary mission of ethical hacking is to enhance cybersecurity defenses and protect digital assets, it must be done while respecting individuals' privacy rights. In this section, we explore the complexities of balancing privacy and security in ethical hacking and the ethical considerations that guide these endeavors.

1. Protecting Sensitive Data:

Ethical hackers often encounter sensitive data during security assessments, including personally identifiable information (PII), financial records, and intellectual property. Respecting privacy means safeguarding this information and ensuring that it is handled securely and confidentially during the testing process.

2. Informed Consent and Authorization:

Before engaging in any security assessments, ethical hackers must obtain informed consent and proper authorization from the organization or individual owning the systems. This process is crucial in ensuring that ethical hacking activities align with legal and ethical standards and do not infringe on privacy rights.

3. Minimizing Data Collection:

Ethical hackers must adopt a "minimize data" approach, ensuring that they only collect the necessary data required for security assessments. Unnecessary data collection could increase privacy risks and expose sensitive information, compromising individuals' privacy.

4. Anonymization and Pseudonymization:

When reporting vulnerabilities or security issues, ethical hackers must employ anonymization or pseudonymization techniques to protect the identity of affected individuals. This ensures that privacy is upheld while still addressing security concerns.

5. Protecting User Privacy in Social Engineering Tests:

Social engineering tests are an essential part of ethical hacking, but they must be conducted with utmost care to protect user privacy. Ethical hackers must avoid collecting personal information or sensitive data during social engineering engagements.

6. Secure Data Disposal:

Once a security assessment is complete, ethical hackers must ensure secure data disposal practices. This includes the proper deletion of any sensitive information collected during the testing process to prevent unauthorized access or data breaches.

7. Privacy Impact Assessments:

Ethical hackers can conduct privacy impact assessments alongside security assessments to identify potential privacy risks and develop appropriate mitigation strategies. This process helps ensure that privacy concerns are addressed proactively throughout the engagement.

8. Ethical Considerations in Vulnerability Disclosure:

When disclosing vulnerabilities, ethical hackers must consider the impact on privacy, especially when it involves public disclosure. Responsible disclosure practices should aim to strike a balance between protecting security and minimizing any negative privacy implications.

9. Continuous Education on Privacy and Security:

Ethical hackers must continually educate themselves on privacy regulations, best practices, and emerging technologies. By staying informed, they can navigate the complexities of privacy and security more effectively in their ethical hacking endeavors.

In conclusion, striking the balance between privacy and security is an ongoing challenge in the ethical hacking community. Ethical hackers must navigate complex ethical considerations to protect individuals' privacy rights while contributing to enhanced cybersecurity defenses. Respecting privacy through informed consent, data minimization, and secure data disposal is paramount. Anonymization and pseudonymization techniques protect individuals' identities during vulnerability disclosure, and privacy impact assessments help identify potential risks. Ethical hackers must continually prioritize education on privacy and security to ensure their actions align with ethical and legal standards. By upholding privacy rights while actively working to bolster cybersecurity defenses, ethical hackers play a vital role in building a digital landscape that is both secure and respectful of individuals' privacy.

Conclusion

A. Reflections on the Journey of Ethical Hacking

The journey of ethical hacking has been nothing short of transformative in the realm of cybersecurity. As we conclude this exploration into the world of ethical hacking, it is essential to reflect on the significant impact ethical hackers have had on securing the digital landscape and the evolving challenges they face.

Ethical hacking has emerged as a crucial pillar in defending against cyber threats. The dedication and expertise of ethical hackers have been instrumental in identifying vulnerabilities, enhancing security measures, and safeguarding sensitive data. The commitment of the global ethical hacking community to using their skills for good have contributed significantly to strengthening the security posture of organizations worldwide.

Throughout this journey, ethical hackers have faced numerous challenges and ethical dilemmas. From navigating legal and regulatory concerns to balancing the delicate relationship between privacy and security, ethical hackers constantly navigate complex ethical considerations. The evolving nature of technology has introduced new ethical challenges, such as the use of AI and automation, deepfakes, and dual-use technologies. Nevertheless, the ethical hacking community has demonstrated resilience and adaptability in addressing these dilemmas responsibly.

Ethical hackers' dedication to responsible disclosure and the promotion of security awareness has fostered a culture of transparency and collaboration within the cybersecurity landscape. Through their efforts, ethical hackers have encouraged organizations to adopt proactive defense strategies, prioritize cybersecurity education, and engage in collaborative threat intelligence sharing. As a result, the entire cybersecurity ecosystem has become more robust and better equipped to defend against cyber threats.

The future of ethical hacking holds great promise and opportunity. As technology continues to advance, ethical hackers will play a critical role in securing emerging technologies like IoT, cloud, and blockchain. They will need to adapt their skills and approaches to address the evolving cyber threat landscape and maintain the ethical principles that guide their actions.

As we move forward, it is essential for ethical hackers to continue their pursuit of knowledge and stay informed about the latest trends and developments in cybersecurity. The ethical hacking community's commitment to continuous learning and professional development will be essential in shaping the future of cybersecurity defense.

In conclusion, the journey of ethical hacking has been a remarkable one, marked by dedication, innovation, and a commitment to securing the digital world. Ethical hackers' contributions to cybersecurity have been invaluable, and their ethical conduct has set a positive example for the entire industry. As we face new challenges in the evolving digital landscape, the global ethical hacking community must continue to uphold ethical principles and strive for a safer and more secure digital future for all. By doing so, ethical hackers will continue to be at the forefront of defending against cyber threats and protecting the digital assets and privacy of individuals and organizations worldwide.

B. Emphasizing the Importance of Ethical Hacking in Securing the Future

In the ever-evolving digital landscape, the importance of ethical hacking cannot be overstated. As we conclude this exploration into the world of ethical hacking, it is crucial to underscore its significance in securing the future of cybersecurity and protecting our interconnected world.

Ethical hacking serves as a formidable line of defense against cyber threats. By adopting the mindset of a potential attacker, ethical hackers identify vulnerabilities and weaknesses that malicious actors could exploit. This proactive approach allows organizations to fortify their defenses, patch vulnerabilities, and implement robust security measures, ultimately reducing the risk of successful cyberattacks.

The impact of cyber threats on individuals, businesses, and governments is far-reaching. Data breaches, financial fraud, and identity theft have become all too common in today's digital landscape. Ethical hacking acts as a powerful deterrent, deterring cybercriminals and mitigating the damage caused by cyber incidents. By strengthening cybersecurity defenses, ethical hacking helps protect sensitive data, intellectual property, and critical infrastructure.

In an era of rapidly advancing technology, the role of ethical hacking extends beyond traditional IT systems. The Internet of Things (IoT), cloud computing, blockchain, and other emerging technologies require specialized security expertise. Ethical hackers are at the forefront of identifying vulnerabilities in these cutting-edge technologies, ensuring they are deployed securely and without compromising user safety.

Moreover, ethical hacking is not just about identifying vulnerabilities but also fostering a culture of security awareness. Ethical hackers advocate for cybersecurity education at all levels, from individuals to organizations.

By empowering users with the knowledge to recognize and respond to cyber threats, ethical hacking creates a more resilient digital ecosystem.

One of the defining features of ethical hacking is responsible disclosure. Ethical hackers adhere to ethical and legal guidelines when disclosing vulnerabilities to organizations, allowing them to patch and remediate before malicious actors can exploit them. This responsible approach to vulnerability disclosure is essential in maintaining a balance between security and privacy.

The future of ethical hacking holds immense potential. As cyber threats continue to evolve, ethical hackers will remain indispensable in countering sophisticated attack vectors. Their adaptability to emerging technologies and dedication to continuous learning will ensure that ethical hacking remains a dynamic and impactful force in cybersecurity.

In conclusion, ethical hacking is a cornerstone of cybersecurity defense and plays a pivotal role in securing the future of our digital world. By proactively identifying vulnerabilities, promoting security awareness, and advocating for responsible disclosure, ethical hackers serve as guardians of our digital safety. As technology advances and cyber threats evolve, the importance of ethical hacking will only grow, making it essential for organizations and governments to recognize its value and invest in the expertise of ethical hackers. By emphasizing the importance of ethical hacking and supporting the global ethical hacking community, we can collectively build a safer and more secure digital future for generations to come.

C. Encouraging Responsible Participation in the World of Ethical Hacking

As we draw to a close on our journey into the world of ethical hacking, it is imperative to emphasize the significance of responsible participation in this dynamic and impactful field. Ethical hacking offers a unique opportunity for individuals to contribute positively to cybersecurity and protect the digital landscape. In this concluding section, we encourage and highlight the importance of responsible participation in the world of ethical hacking.

1. Embracing Ethical and Legal Boundaries:

Responsible participation in ethical hacking starts with a thorough understanding of ethical and legal boundaries. Ethical hackers must abide by laws and regulations related to cybersecurity, ensuring that their actions are always conducted within the confines of legality and ethical standards.

2. Acquiring Proper Training and Certifications:

Ethical hacking demands specialized skills and knowledge. Aspiring ethical hackers should invest in comprehensive training programs and obtain relevant certifications from reputable organizations. Formal education and certifications ensure that ethical hackers possess the necessary expertise to conduct security assessments responsibly.

3. Promoting Responsible Disclosure Practices:

Ethical hackers should prioritize responsible vulnerability disclosure. Timely and coordinated disclosure helps organizations address vulnerabilities before they can be exploited by malicious actors. It is essential for ethical hackers to communicate with affected parties in a constructive and respectful manner.

4. Contributing to Open-Source Projects:

Participating in open-source projects within the cybersecurity community fosters collaboration and knowledge sharing. Ethical hackers can contribute to the development of security tools, share insights, and engage with fellow professionals to strengthen the collective defense against cyber threats.

5. Staying Abreast of Emerging Trends:

The field of cybersecurity is constantly evolving. Ethical hackers must commit to continuous learning and stay up-to-date with emerging trends, new attack vectors, and evolving defense mechanisms. Being informed enables ethical hackers to remain effective and relevant in securing the ever-changing digital landscape.

6. Engaging in Bug Bounty Programs:

Bug bounty programs provide ethical hackers with opportunities to apply their skills to real-world scenarios while earning rewards for responsibly disclosing vulnerabilities. Participating in bug bounty programs promotes responsible hacking practices and strengthens security across industries.

7. Emphasizing Ethical Conduct:

Ethical hackers must prioritize ethical conduct in their interactions with clients, peers, and the broader cybersecurity community. Upholding professionalism, integrity, and honesty are essential to building trust and credibility within the industry.

8. Promoting Security Awareness:

Responsible ethical hackers should actively advocate for security awareness among individuals and organizations. By educating users about cybersecurity best practices and potential risks, ethical hackers empower others to play an active role in protecting their digital assets.

9. Nurturing an Ethical Hacking Community:

Ethical hacking thrives in a supportive and collaborative community. Ethical hackers should foster an environment that encourages knowledge sharing, mentorship, and a commitment to ethical principles. A strong community elevates the impact and influence of ethical hacking in the broader cybersecurity landscape.

In conclusion, responsible participation in the world of ethical hacking is critical for ensuring the positive impact of this essential field. By embracing ethical and legal boundaries, acquiring proper training, and promoting responsible disclosure practices, ethical hackers can contribute significantly to cybersecurity. Engaging in open-source projects, staying informed about emerging trends, and participating in bug bounty programs further strengthens ethical hacking practices. Emphasizing ethical conduct and promoting security awareness are fundamental in fostering a secure digital ecosystem. By nurturing a supportive ethical hacking community, ethical hackers can collectively shape the future of cybersecurity defense, safeguarding the digital world for generations to come. Through responsible participation, ethical hackers are true agents of positive change, safeguarding our digital future one step at a time.